THE FLOOD OF MERCY

Supernatural Help
In Your Greatest Time Of Need

THE FLOOD OF MERCY

Supernatural Help
In Your Greatest Time Of Need

ROSE RAMANDI

All emphasis within Scripture quotation is the author's own. Unless otherwise noted, all references from the concordance are taken from Blue Letter Bible - https://www.blueletterbible.org

International Standard Book Number (ISBN) for print copy: 978-1-9995000-0-9

ISBN for E-book: 978-1-9995000-1-6

Visit the Author's website at: http://www.perfectedbyblood.com

Dedication

I dedicate this, my first book, to the One whose heart beats are like the sound of many oceans where I can hear the waves of His love rising up to roar; the One whose eyes of fire are the place where the reflection of His heart is seen; the One who when I first gazed upon Him, fully captured my heart and transformed me with the power of His love; and the One who has become the only true meaning and purpose of my life. He who is the One that is my hope and whose Mercy is without limit, my Lord and Savior - "Jesus Christ".

Acknowledgments

I wish to express my deepest appreciation to my husband, Masoud Ramandi, for his constant support, amazing encouragement and wonderful advice during this journey which enabled me to make my vision a reality. I would not have been able to accomplish this without you, my love!

I also want to thank Laurie Paul for helping me edit this book, in preparation for its publishing. Your selfless work during the compilation of my transcript is truly priceless. You are amazing.

Table of Contents

Introduction

It was the Tuesday after the Thanksgiving weekend. I went to work very refreshed and excited as I had spent the whole weekend with Jesus, reading the Bible and enjoying His presence.

When I got to work that morning, I was full of life - singing and dancing - awakened my co-workers who were all still yawning! Once seated at my desk, I turned my computer on and began checking my emails. As I opened the first email and started to read it, my heart began beating faster. The email was from a customer informing us that their entire shipment had been received with incorrect products in it. I was suddenly gripped with panic and fear; I could not believe what I was reading. I ran to the archive cabinet and pulled out the original order that I had entered a few months prior. I grew quiet as I returned to my desk and started to check the customer's order. While comparing it with my original order entry form, I found that I had, indeed, entered the wrong customer product in the system. This order was one of the biggest sales for the month and, regrettably, had already been shipped and delivered to the customer.

The product that was shipped had become obsolete a few years prior and was of no use to the customer. As such, the customer wanted the incorrect order sent back to our facility and the correct product shipped back to them immediately, overnight. Correcting the shipment error would inevitably mean additional overnight production charges, shipping costs and potential penalty charge due to interruption in the customer's production line.

I took a deep breath! I could hear and feel my heartbeat in my chest. I had never made that kind of error before in my career. I quickly re-checked the system to see if I could find an explanation or rationale that I could use to "defend" my error to upper management, but there was none!

Fearful, I ran to my car and I cried out:

"Jesus have Mercy on me! Help me, Lord. I did not do this intentionally. I receive your Mercy in this situation. Your Mercy triumphs over every judgment of the flesh, over every error and mistake. I am not the victim of my own mistakes. Your blood washes my mistakes away. Your Mercy causes me not to live in the consequences of my errors. Have Mercy on me".

I continued talking to Jesus, reminding Him (better to say, reminding myself) who He really is and what He has done for me until I finally felt peace!

Before going back to my office, I decided that I would not attempt to defend myself; I knew Jesus would do so on my behalf.

As soon as I got back to my desk feeling totally at peace, my boss immediately summoned me to her office. The customer's email had also been sent to her as well. My boss was clearly not happy about the situation and proceeded to ask me about it. I replied: "I have already checked all the backup documents; it was my order entry error".

My boss began to panic. Her department's performance was in jeopardy, not to mention a significant financial loss for the company.

I started returning to my desk not knowing what was going to happen next. By the time I got to my desk, I saw yet another email about the error; but this one had come from the involved sales representative. I could not believe what I was reading! The sales representative had just emailed my manager to apologize for the mistake, indicating that the error was "hers" not mine and that my boss, as well as the company, should record the error as hers alone because she had not double checked the order in the system.

Why would she do that? This was clearly my fault. It was not her responsibility to double check the order to ensure it was entered correctly. Then I thought to myself: "Wow! Maybe this is what Mercy does!". But as I was thinking this to myself, I heard the Lord say to me:

"No, this is not Mercy! Mercy does not put blame on someone else to make another free. Now get up and go to your manager and make it very clear to her that it was your mistake and not someone else's".

I paused for a moment: "hmmm.... Lord, is this you?".

I knew it was the Lord, so I went to my manager's office and told her: "This mistake was not due to the sales representative's error. It was due to my error. All of the documentation proves that it was clearly my mistake. I just want to ensure that you understand that she is blameless!". My manager replied by simply saying: "Okay".

I returned to my desk with multiple thoughts going through my mind: "Rose, do you know what you are doing? People all over the world gather evidence, even falsify evidence, to defend themselves and prove their lack of guilt. But instead, you have just chosen to insist and offer proof that the error was yours alone! What have you done? You will surely be in trouble!".

As these thoughts were going through my mind, I heard myself answering back: "Yes, you got that right. I do not defend myself - He does!". All worries then left my mind and I was once again back to my dancing and singing mood, waiting to see what Mercy will do! Obviously, this was not understandable for my co-workers, who knew what had been transpiring.

A few hours later, as I was coming back from my lunch break, I saw my boss coming out of her office, almost dancing! She appeared to be very excited. She called me to her office and said: "Did you see the new email from the sales rep?". "No", I replied, "I just came back from lunch". She happily continued, "Well, the customer has emailed me back to advise that she was looking at her inventory and realized that they were very low on some products. They had had a fire in their plant a couple of months prior, which resulted in the loss of some products. They have determined that they can use the products that we sent to them in error. Even though the products were obsolete, they can still be used to keep their production line running! We do not need to return the obsolete products after all, nor pay any penalty. In fact, they will be paying us for all of it! They do, however, want us to produce the correct products as well, and ship them as soon as possible".

Upon hearing this news, I was both shocked and excited, and thought to myself: "Oh wow, Mercy!".

My manager laughed and continued by saying: "Well, thank you for making more money for the company! I like these kinds of mistakes!". "You are most welcome!", I replied.

I smiled and left her office thinking to myself: "What just happened? Everyone who was involved in this mistake of mine, instead of getting hurt by it, benefitted from it! The customer was happy because the error topped up their inventory that was low due to a fire, enabling them to keep their production line running. My boss was happy because her department made a profit. The company was happy because they did not need to pay any additional penalty or shipping charges, nor scrap a huge amount of product and lose money as a result. I was happy now because the error worked out to be in my favour after all, and did not cause me any trouble at work".

This is what only Mercy can do!

My story above is but one of many similar stories that has happened to me since that time. While other mistakes have not been as big, the underlying principle still remains the same: "Mercy triumphs over Judgment". James says:

13 For judgment is without Mercy to the one who has shown no Mercy. Mercy triumphs over judgment. [James 2:13]

As the "victim" of my many past mistakes, I had to "endure" the consequences for years and years. But once I began to understand and realize what Mercy truly is, things in my life began happening in my favour.

In this book, I will share some of the understanding around the subject of Mercy by using the word of God and interpreting one scripture with another, in order to ensure that we have a complete and accurate understanding of the scriptures as a whole.

It is my hope that this book unveils this prevailing attribute of God in your hearts and causes you to believe, profoundly, in His Mercy in your life like never before; thereby raising you up, such that you will never again become the victim of your weaknesses and mistakes. Amen!

An Overview of Mercy

9 Who has saved us and called [us] with a holy calling, not according to our works, but according to His own purpose and grace which was given to us in Christ Jesus before time began. [2 Timothy 1:9]

Everything that comes to us is only by God's grace. This grace was given to us "before time began" and originated entirely from the One who says "I AM". It is His great love that causes Him to be compassionate toward us and come to our aid when we are weak. He chose to create mankind in His own likeness; to be in His own image and to be His children. In the same sense, earthly parents do not treat their children solely based on their children's performance; at least not those who have some degree of sensibility!

In today's so-called "common" understanding, "Mercy" is often defined as "not getting what you deserve". Even though it seems a reasonable definition in the beginning, it is not a grace-based understanding, which overlooks the love of God. It also ignores how God introduces Himself, even throughout the Old Testament, especially to Moses:

5 Now the LORD descended in the cloud and stood with him there and proclaimed the name of the LORD. 6 And the LORD passed before him and proclaimed, "The LORD, the LORD God, Merciful and gracious, longsuffering, and abounding in goodness and truth." [Exodus 34:5-6]

Even though this common description of Mercy seems to be logical, it is not scriptural; it robs the children of God from the depth of the kindness of their loving Father. Only those who have a lack of something hesitate to give to another. God is not poor, but rather, is rich in everything. He is the One who created all things and yet came to man[1] and told him that he could have it all. Moreover, he must rule over all of it.

God's riches were meant to be transferred to man, but man's blindness to the goodness of this loving Father caused man to separate himself from the Father. Man separated himself from God by way of the "covering" he made for himself. Man did so by choosing to eat from the strength of his own flesh and doing all according to his own fleshly wisdom – a wisdom he had inherited from the serpent. By way of his choices, man turned his back on the One who created and loved him.

This story is true to this day, but the truth can change it. The apostle Paul writes to the church at Ephesus:

4 But God, who is rich in Mercy, because of His great love with which He loved us, 5 even when we were dead in trespasses, made us alive together with Christ (by grace you have been saved), 6 and raised [us] up together, and made [us] sit together in the heavenly [places] in Christ Jesus, 7 that in the ages to come He might show the exceeding riches of His grace in [His] kindness toward us in Christ Jesus. [Ephesians 2:4-7]

God is rich in Mercy! It was His great "love" that caused His Mercy to come to us, not our wretchedness! Because of His great love, He shows us Mercy, so He can then show us the exceeding riches of His grace.

---

[1] "Man" in this book refers to mankind, both male and female. Genesis 1:27 says that God created man in His own image, male and female.

The Adamic mind is so wired to legalism that it still struggles to embrace the heart of God as the Father. It thinks there should be a reason why one should receive goodness and yet God has been shouting for thousands of years: "Adam, where are you?". It is not that God did not or does not know where man was or is. Rather, God calls man to shake him from the drunkenness of darkness, from living under condemnation and from thinking that he must measure up and fix himself. By way of His love and Mercifulness, God removes the "covering" that man has made for himself and then "clothes" man with Himself. We see this prophesy in Genesis 3:21 where God made a covering for man:

> *21 Also, for Adam and his wife the LORD God made tunics of skin and clothed them. [Genesis 3:21]*

While man tried to cover himself with fig leaves because of the shame of his nakedness, God reached out to him with His own covering. This was a prophetic picture of His ultimate plan for mankind, as repeatedly revealed in New Testament scriptures:

> *13 Let us walk properly, as in the day, not in revelry and drunkenness, not in lewdness and lust, not in strife and envy. 14 But put on the Lord Jesus Christ, and make no provision for the flesh, to fulfill its lusts. [Romans 13:13-14]*

In this verse, the apostle Paul is not saying, "You shall not be a drunkard". (This they knew from the law of Moses in the Old Testament). Rather, Paul is trying to say that if we, as believers of Christ, do not know who we are in Christ, it is as if we are drunk; yet not with the new wine of the Spirit, but with the old wine. In verse 11 he exhorts the church to "awake":

> *11 And [do] this, knowing the time, that now [it is] high time to awake out of sleep; for now, our salvation [is] nearer than when we [first] believed. [Romans 13:11]*

Certainly, Paul does not mean awaking in a natural sense! The context is righteousness, our identity and who we are in Christ. That is why he tells us, in verse 14, to "put on Christ". A better translation reads: "Clothe yourselves with Christ".

This was God's plan, since the creation of man; that we would not live on our own hand-made provision, but rather, rely on His love and drink from His goodness that causes us to always remain in a place of "repentance" – meaning, out of our mind, but in the mind of Christ. Only then can we bear His fruit, the fruit of the Spirit; and only then can we manifest His image and His likeness.

By far we understand that the origin of Mercy is love. It is because of His great love that He shows us Mercy.

The error in understanding "Mercy" is not made willingly, but most probably was initiated because of the language difficulties caused when a word from one language is translated to another. In some cases, the Greek or Hebrew word does not exist in English, and therefore, the translator uses the closest word that could convey its original meaning. Consequently, when readers read the Bible, each time they see that word, they understand it through the filter of the translated word and the depth or meaning of what the Lord has intended to be conveyed could be lost. Having said this, by looking at the context, and with the help of the Holy Spirit, we can fully comprehend the depth of the words, as He reveals it to us.

Even if the translators might have picked the closest word for each original word, we still need to understand the vocabulary of the Bible, by finding out its definition according to the Bible's vocabulary. This way, we have a correct definition for each word and can then understand the Bible in a more accurate way.

In this book, the Mercy of God, God's powerful nature will be unveiled. Mercy comes to us continually, as part of mankind, until we are each "convicted" of His love and are thus "conformed" to what each of us were predestined for. With this in mind, we will go through scriptures to show that "Mercy" is an action originating from the nature of God, intended to help man in his weaknesses; bringing salvation in the time of need and "delivering" man, when man cannot help himself.

David cries out in his sixth Psalm:

> *2 Have Mercy on me, O LORD, for I [am] weak; O LORD, heal me, for my bones are troubled. [Psalm 6:2]*

And,

> *4 Return, O LORD, deliver me! Oh, save me for Your Mercies' sake! [Psalm 6:4]*

Mercy, An Everlasting Covenant

The surest way to understand the meaning of a word in the Bible is to look at the context of where that word is being used in scripture. The word "Mercy" (Checed - Strong's H2617) is used 248 times in the Old Testament in the King James translation, of which 127 times is in the book of Psalms. This suggests that Psalms is a major book in the understanding of "Mercy". It also shows us that David, who is one of the writers of Psalms, had a profound revelation of "Mercy"! With this, we can better understand why people who came to Jesus, calling Him Son of David, asked for Mercy saying: "Jesus, Son of David, have Mercy on us". In their understanding of the scriptures, Son of David was the one who had "Sure Mercy". For this reason, everyone who asked Jesus for Mercy received what they desired. Later, this became fully revealed by Paul, when he preached about Jesus to the Jews in Acts chapter 13:

> *34 And that He raised Him from the dead, no more to return to corruption, He has spoken thus: "I will give you the Sure Mercies of David." [Acts 13:34]*

This verse is quoted from Isaiah 55 when Isaiah, by the Spirit of God, prophesied of the new covenant[2] that would come through the Son of David:

> *3 Incline your ear, and come to Me. Hear, and your soul shall live; and I will make an everlasting covenant with you – The Sure Mercies of David. [Isaiah 55:3]*

There were many written prophesies, through various prophets, that the one who would bring salvation for mankind would be from the seed of David, thus having the "Sure Mercies of David". When Jesus came to earth, He came as the "seed of David"[3].

Many realized this truth about Jesus while He was on earth. They knew He had come according to the Sure Mercies of David and they, therefore, knew this Mercy was "sure". The word "sure" is translated as "Faithful" in other places in the New Testament, thus indicating His seriousness about "Mercy" and assurance that He is willing to provide it for those who need it.

When the scripture speaks of an "everlasting covenant", it means that there will be no change to the covenant once it is established. For example, the presence of Jesus on earth was the fulfilment of time for people in order to leave the old behind and enter into the new; this fulfilment is an "everlasting covenant".

On the other hand, Isaiah 55:3 says: *"I will make a covenant…"*, the indication of "I will" shows us that there will be an end to the old covenant and the bringing of a new covenant that will be "everlasting". In this particular case, the old covenant that had to pass away was not based on the "Sure Mercies of David". For this reason, it had to be changed to a new everlasting, ever-remaining, covenant of "Mercy". The new "everlasting covenant" would be according to God's own Mercy - a Mercy toward man that is everlasting, with no end and with no change.

---

2 Or New Testament

3 Refer to Matthew 1:1, Romans 1:3 and 2 Timothy 2:8

The passing away of the old covenant was necessary because it was established on the works of the law, not grace. What remains, is the new covenant that is established on Mercy according to God's grace and not on the works of the law. Paul writes in His letter to the Romans that the one who does the works of the law shall live by the law:

5 For Moses writes about the righteousness which is of the law, "The man who does those things shall live by them." [Romans 10:5]

And then he adds that if we live by the law, it is not of grace. If it is by grace, it is no longer of the works of the law:

6 And if by grace, then [it is] no longer of works; otherwise grace is no longer grace. But if [it is] of works, it is no longer grace; otherwise work is no longer work. [Romans 11:6]

Therefore, it has to be either by law or by grace. It cannot be both. The old covenant, which was of the law and not of grace, had to come to an end. This is because that by the works of the law no flesh is justified in the sight of God[4].

The covenant between God and man must not be according to the abilities and works of man, but rather, according to God's abilities, work, and nature toward man. What man has been striving to have, which has been the plan of God for mankind since creation, is not attainable by the works of man's hand. It comes by His Power and Spirit. Down through the ages and generations, the works of the law - man's own power and his abilities - have not been able to give man life. In other words, the complete redemption from the corruption and decay of his own body.

As we read in Galatians chapter 3:

21 [Is] the law then against the promises of God? Certainly not! For if there had been a law given which could have given life, truly righteousness would have been by the law. [Galatians 3:21]

---

[4] Romans 3:20

From the beginning of time, God planned life for mankind; the works of man's hand or the works of the law cannot fulfill His plan! Rather, there would have to be an alternate way to bring salvation for mankind which is why a saviour, someone who is beyond our own ability and power, had to come and stretch out a hand toward us and deliver us from the swamp of corruption. This is also why God, through the mouth of many prophets, prophesied of the "coming of the One" who will put an end to the old covenant, which was ministering death to man, thus bringing a new covenant that ministers life.[5]

This new covenant brings life to man because it is not based on man's labour, intellect, achievements nor deeds. Rather, it is given freely to man according to the richness of His grace and His Mercy!

This is why some people, during the time when Jesus was on earth, cried out to Him for Mercy and received what they had asked for, without performing a single act. Some of these people were not even Jews, but foreigners - Samaritans and Canaanites. This covenant was not and is not limited only to a certain group of people, but rather, extends to all mankind. People recognized that Jesus was the One who was to be the Saviour and, therefore, the One who could save mankind through His Mercy; a Mercy that is everlasting, never changing and never ending!

These people did not know of any reasons why they would not be helped by Jesus; they all had reasons why He would help them. If we read their stories in the gospels of the New Testament, we realize that most of them encountered something that could have potentially stopped them from receiving His Mercy. However, each time any form of discouragement got in the way of their request, they raised their voices even higher, insisting that "Mercy" be given to them!

Let us take a look at a couple of these stories to understand how they demonstrated a Mercy-based mindset:

---

[5] 2 Corinthians 3:6-11

THE CANAANITE WOMAN [MATTHEW 15:22-28]

*22 And behold, a woman of Canaan came from that region and cried out to Him, saying, "**Have Mercy on me, O Lord, Son of David!** My daughter is severely demon-possessed."*

23 But He answered her not a word. And His disciples came and urged Him, saying, "Send her away, for she cries out after us."

24 But He answered and said, "I was not sent except to the lost sheep of the house of Israel."

*25 Then she came and worshiped Him, saying, "**Lord, help me!**"*

26 But He answered and said, "It is not good to take the children's bread and throw it to the little dogs."

27 And she said, "Yes, Lord, yet even the little dogs eat the crumbs which fall from their masters' table."

28 Then Jesus answered and said to her, "O woman, great is your faith! Let it be to you as you desire." And her daughter was healed from that very hour. [Matthew 15:22-28]

This Canaanite woman needed the kind of help that could only come from one person: Jesus; the One who had the "Sure Mercies of David" as an everlasting covenant. In verse 22, she calls unto Jesus asking Him to have Mercy on her. Yet, in verse 25, she asks for help! She understood that Mercy is a "help" that comes to the one who needs help. It is not contained in a deserving-based mindset, but rather, is an action of the strong helping the weak. Strong's Concordance defines Mercy as:

> *The kindness and goodwill toward the afflicted or weak, joint with a desire and action to help them.*

The "weak" is someone like this mother who was desperate, helpless and hopeless. She could not help her daughter, nor could anyone else, except through His Mercy. But surprisingly, when she came to Jesus asking for Mercy, she did not receive what she had wanted at first. She had to persist on receiving it and relinquish all other reasoning, which was contrary to what she needed:

First, Jesus did not say a word when she was crying out asking for Mercy: *"But He answered her not a word"*. Then the disciples came to Jesus asking Him to send her away: *"Send her away, for she cries out after us"*. Then Jesus replied: *"I was not sent except to the lost sheep of the house of Israel"*. But the woman, still persisting while ignoring all reasons that were against hope, fell before Jesus and worshipped Him. Jesus again rejected her request by saying: *"It is not good to take the children's bread and throw it to the little dogs"*. Yet again, the woman remained determined not to leave until she got the Mercy and the help that she needed, steadfast in her reasons for why she must obtain healing for her daughter:

> *27 And she said, "Yes, Lord, yet even the little dogs eat the crumbs which fall from their masters' table." [Matthew 15:27]*

She was so persuaded and determined that she did not get upset when she was compared to little dogs, but rather, reasoned further in her reply that can be interpreted to mean: "You are correct, but I am Your dog and You need to take care of me!".

This story happened before Jesus' crucifixion and that is why Jesus told her: *"I was not sent except to the lost sheep of the house of Israel"* or even saying: *"It is not good to take the children's bread and throw it to the little dogs"*. Jesus came forth from Israel to bring salvation to all mankind, including Gentiles and this woman. He came as the seed of David, an Israelite, and was sent to Israel first so that they would reject and crucify Him. Through this, He would become the "stone" that was rejected by the "builders" of the law (Israel) and could then become the stone of foundation for another building, which is not by the law, but by grace. For it is by grace that the Gentiles (like this woman) could come into the house of God, be the children of the house of God, and receive the bread and the inheritance of their Father.

The story of the Gentile Canaanite-Woman happened before the crucifixion of Jesus and His rejection by Israel. The woman persisted on receiving something that was going to be available for her in the future, but not yet at that time! However, David had written in multiple places in his Psalms that: *"His Mercy endures forever"* or *"His Mercy is everlasting"*. With this being the case, receiving His Mercy is not bound by time; it can be obtained at anytime by faith. It is therefore by faith that the woman reached out to receive Mercy when she needed it, even though the time for the Gentiles had not yet arrived.

> *28 Then Jesus answered and said to her, "O woman, great is your faith! Let it be to you as you desire." And her daughter was healed from that very hour. [Matthew 15:28]*

Therefore, all that is required to dive deep into the Mercy of the Lord is faith and not good deeds or genealogies!

THE BLIND BARTIMAEUS [MARK 10:46-52]

Let us now look at another story about a person who, in a similar fashion, was persuaded of the availability of Mercy and persisted to receive it:

> *46 Now they came to Jericho. As He went out of Jericho with His disciples and a great multitude, blind Bartimaeus, the son of Timaeus, sat by the road begging.*
>
> *47 And when he heard that it was Jesus of Nazareth, he began to cry out and say, "Jesus, Son of David, have Mercy on me!"*
>
> *48 Then many warned him to be quiet; but he cried out all the more, "Son of David, have Mercy on me!"[Mark 10:46-48]*

"Bartimaeus" means "Son of Timaeus", with "Timaeus" meaning "unclean". His name was "Son of unclean"! This man was blind, a beggar, and sitting at the gate of a city called "Jericho".

Jericho was a city that Joshua, years beforehand, had entered into when he was taking the children of Israel from the wilderness to the promise land. Jericho was the first city on their way. God had instructed Joshua to make people march around the city for seven days, followed by shouting on the last day at the hearing of the trumpet. In doing so, the walls of the city fell flat[6]! And now Bartimaeus was in the same city and he needed to bring the walls down. This time the walls were the voices of people, which had risen, warning him to be quiet and drowning out his voice from Jesus!

He could not get up to go look for Jesus like everyone else, otherwise, he would be trampled underfoot of the crowds who were also out looking for Jesus. All he could do was remain where he was, raise his voice, and call unto Jesus.

At first, Bartimaeus shouted, but many came to him and warned him to be quiet! Quite possibly, he may have also been threatened for what he was doing! Perhaps he was even mocked, beaten, and disregarded by people and warned many times before this incident as well! Unfortunately, he was a beggar, not honourable in the sight of men, considered unclean and rejected by them. But this time was different for him. He knew the Sure Mercy of David was passing by and for this reason, he must get the help that no one could give, except Mercy! As more time passed, possibly the crowd kept getting bigger, louder, and denser. Bartimaeus knew that he had to raise his voice louder and higher than everyone else around him so that Jesus could hear his voice through the noise of the crowd. Instead of being discouraged, he raised his voice high, loud like a trumpet, higher than the other voices, crying out even more: "Son of David, have Mercy on me!".

Then Jesus heard him amidst all other voices! The rest of the story is as follows:

> *49 So Jesus stood still and commanded him to be called. Then they called the blind man, saying to him, "Be of good cheer. Rise, He is calling you."*
>
> *50 And throwing aside his garment, he rose and came to Jesus.*

---

[6] Joshua 6:1-20

51 So Jesus answered and said to him, "What do you want me to do for you?" The blind man said to Him, "Rabboni, that I may receive my sight."

52 Then Jesus said to him, "Go your way; your faith has made you well." And immediately he received his sight and followed Jesus on the road. [Mark 10:49-52]

Blind Bartimaeus stayed where he was until he was called by Jesus. Until then, all he had been able to do was to cry out as loud as possible to be heard. Once he was called by Jesus, he threw away his garment and came to Jesus. He came to Jesus with nothing in his hand. He did not even bring what he had achieved through his own way of living.

The interesting part of this story for me is that as soon as he came to Jesus, it was Jesus who asked him: "What do you want Me to do for you?". Unlike many occasions in our lives in which we wonder and ask God: "What do I need to do?", this man instead realized that there was nothing He could do to attain, achieve, nor receive his sight. There was only one thing that could heal him, His Sure Mercy. He even threw away the only thing he had, his garment.

The blind man answered Jesus' question: *"Rabboni, that I may receive my sight".* He called Him "Rabboni" which means "teacher". But we know that it is not a teacher who can heal the sick, but rather, a doctor. Nevertheless, this blind man called Jesus a teacher and yet asked for the opening of His eyes. He must have heard His teachings prior to that event, either from others or even when he was amongst the crowds. Hearing His teachings first opened the eyes of his understanding and he realized that anything received from God is only because of His Mercy. Hence, His teachings developed an assurance of heart in him, thus causing him to have faith to endure every opposition and in the end, to receive his sight.

This man, by calling Jesus "teacher" and asking to receive his sight, demonstrated a powerful truth: "His teachings are eye-opening". His teachings open our eyes to see that this is He who has Mercy on us; that this is He who asks us: *"what can I do for you?"* and that this is He who wills and also works in us for our good. His teachings first open our eyes to see that this is the Mercy which comes to our aid in the time of need and that we do not need to perform, do something or bring an offering to receive from Him. Rather, we can come to Him boldly with full assurance of heart, knowing that He is Merciful and will help us in the time of need.

There are some similarities between the stories of the Canaanite Woman and Blind Bartimaeus:

They both asked for Mercy because they realized that He was the Son of David and had come according to the Sure Mercy of David. Both encountered something that could have potentially stopped them to receive the help. They persevered through the midst of all of the oppositions because something in them was saying, "His Mercy is sure". In the end, they both were admired by Jesus for their faith and received their healings. Their faith simply was on His Mercy. They believed that His Mercy is indisputable, is for them, and most importantly, that He is willing to show them Mercy. They persisted their way through, bringing reasons to reason out any other dispute that was against them.

This is what a persuaded heart does when His Mercy is counted as the only source of help. We should not let any opposing voice rising up in our hearts make us quiet and stop us from receiving His Mercy. Rather, we must shout even more: "You are Merciful, O Lord, Jesus Son of David, have Mercy on me". We must have a confidence and assurance of heart that His Mercy is His covenant toward us and, therefore, it will not fail. We are the children of the covenant of God and He cannot annul or fail His own covenant when He himself has called it an everlasting covenant:

> *3 Incline your ear, and come to Me. Hear, and your soul shall live; and I will make an everlasting covenant with you—The Sure Mercies of David. [Isaiah 55:3]*

We hear Him who says the everlasting covenant is according to the Sure Mercies of David. It is the Mercy of God toward man and not according to what one may or may not have. That is why the beginning of Isaiah 55 confirms this:

> *1 Ho! Everyone who thirsts, come to the waters; And you who have no money, come, buy and eat. Yes, come, buy wine and milk without money and without price. 2 Why do you spend money for [what is] not bread, and your wages for [what] does not satisfy? Listen carefully to Me, and eat [what is] good, and let your soul delight itself in abundance. [Isaiah 55:1-2]*

Come and buy without money, without price! Not because it is cheap, but instead, because it is so valuable that it cannot be bought with man's own possessions. It must be given to you as a gift. Since this covenant is according to His Mercy, He then will give it all to us freely, without money, without a price.

Mankind has been spending all of its wealth trying to attain "things" in this life that have never profited mankind and all the while, during these fruitless "self-efforts", God has been crying out since Genesis (when the first man, Adam, failed) to come to Him directly instead.

We do not need to toil, work, or perform to be able to attain and achieve. In fact, it is impossible to attain and achieve with the works of our own hands. We must realize that this is all according to His Mercy. He chose to make a covenant with us that was, and is, in accordance with Sure Mercy. He was so sure about this covenant that He called it an everlasting, un-ending covenant. He was so sure about this covenant because it was not dependent on man, but on God alone.

The only way to come and "eat" what He has prepared for us is to "incline our ears" to hear and to listen carefully to Him. But what is this that we need to hear, give heed and listen carefully to? The next verse answers that question:

> *3 Incline your ear, and come to Me. Hear, and your soul shall live; and I will make an everlasting covenant with you—The Sure Mercies of David. [Isaiah 55:3]*

"I will make an everlasting covenant with you, the Sure Mercies of David", is what we need to listen carefully to. The word "I" is an important word that we should meditate on. It is not the covenant that we have made with God. Rather, it is His covenant, His plan and His desire for us. It is His plan to show us Mercy forever. It is His plan to make a kind of covenant with us that gives us everything without money, without our own possessions, and without our qualifications. This covenant will never change, but we can change the way that we have been thinking. The world, our experiences and many other factors have taught us to think differently than the way God thinks. We have been taught that there is nothing good for free and that things of more value are typically more expensive. But when we come to God, His teachings are entirely different:

> *7 Let the wicked forsake his way, and the unrighteous man <u>his thoughts</u>; Let him <u>return to the LORD</u>, and <u>He will have mercy on him</u>; And to our God, for He will abundantly pardon. [Isaiah 55:7]*

And,

> *8 "For <u>My thoughts</u> [are] not your thoughts, nor [are] your ways <u>My ways</u>," says the LORD. 9 "For [as] the heavens are higher than the earth, so are <u>My ways higher</u> than your ways, and <u>My thoughts</u> than your thoughts." [Isaiah 55:8-9]*

The world does not think "Mercy", but rather, it thinks "Judgment" according to good deeds and bad deeds. The Lord expresses His heart through these verses and tells us that those thoughts are wicked. Everyone who thinks this way is called upon by God to turn their thoughts to His way; to "His Mercy". When our thoughts are changed, our ways are changed, and we receive "Mercy" for He easily pardons us, not holding anything against us. This is all because of the everlasting covenant of Mercy.

The thoughts of the Lord are toward us and in alignment with the Sure Mercies of David, His own covenant. He cannot break His own covenant by thinking otherwise and showing us anything contrary to the covenant. Therefore, His thoughts toward us are always "Mercy" and how He can show us Mercy, His way! That is why the Lord in these verses cries out and asks everyone to turn their thoughts away from worldly thinking, but rather turn to "higher" thoughts - His thoughts; Heavenly thoughts; "MERCY" thoughts.

It is for this reason that we need to incline our ears and listen carefully to His thoughts. We need to turn and start listening to His higher thoughts, not our own thoughts which have been ruling and reigning our lives for years, often dictating our way of living. Rather, by having "Mercy" thoughts, we will find higher ways of living because Mercy is His way of life for us.

All God wants from us is to stop thinking that we need to have something (e.g. money) to bring to God or buy from Him. All He has been saying from the beginning to man is:

"Why are you afraid of Me? Why are you running away from Me? Why are you hiding and struggling to get through life? Let me show you the higher way of living. Let Me embrace you. Come and receive My most valuable things without price, without money. Hear My voice and run to Me. Don't do what your father, Adam, did! Don't hide from Me. Come, I will make a covenant with you so that you are assured of My Mercy and that you may know, with a persuaded heart, that I will never ever change My mind towards you. My covenant will remain and thus, My Mercy is everlasting". Allow His Mercy to guide your thoughts:

> *10 For as the rain comes down, and the snow from heaven, and do not return there, but water the earth, and make it bring forth and bud, that it may give seed to the sower and bread to the eater,*
>
> *11 So shall My word be that goes forth from My mouth; It shall not return to Me void, but it shall accomplish what I please, and it shall prosper [in the thing] for which I sent it.*
>
> *12 For you shall go out with joy and be led out with peace; The mountains and the hills shall break forth into singing before you, and all the trees of the field shall clap [their] hands.*

13 Instead of the thorn shall come up the cypress tree, and instead of the brier shall come up the myrtle tree; And it shall be to the LORD for a name, for an everlasting sign [that] shall not be cut off. [Isaiah 55:10-13]

Mercy, A Burning Passion

The story of Blind Bartimaeus is also recorded, in more detail, in the gospel of Matthew. The gospel of Mathew speaks of two blind men who were sitting at Jericho and calling for Mercy. This gospel finishes the story as follows:

> *34 So Jesus had compassion and touched their eyes. And immediately their eyes received sight, and they followed Him. [Matthew 20:34]*

In the previous chapter, we saw that the blind man cried out for Mercy and, as the result, he received his sight. However, in the gospel of Matthew, we read that while the blind men asked for "Mercy", Jesus had "Compassion" on them and then healed them.

The word used for "Compassion" in the Greek is "splagchnizomai" (G4697) which means, "to be moved as to one's bowels". It comes from the word "bowels" such as the heart, lungs, liver and all internal organs. Basically, the definition of this word is:

"To be moved with passion, a violent and burning passion from every inner part of one".

It is a passion that resides in the heart and every inner organ that causes one to move and show an action. Thus, compassion is an inside movement, something that happens in the heart and every inner part of one's being that moves him to show an action. The action itself is "Mercy".

Blind Bartimaeus asked for Mercy to receive his sight. Jesus had compassion and opened his eyes. The action of Jesus opening Bartimaeus' blind eyes was the "Mercy" shown to him by Jesus. In this story, Jesus was moved with compassion from every inner part of His being. The burning passion inside of His heart, His kidney, every single organ of His inner being moved Him to open the eyes of this blind man.

This is Mercy! It originates from the One who shows it because of the internal burning passion.

The One who is rich in Mercy, our God, is rich in compassion toward us as well. He moves with a burning passion that is within His inner being. His love stirs up this passion, compels Him to take an action and thus showing us Mercy. He is so moved with the burning passion of His own heart that it does not matter to Him whether we deserve it or not. He is not moved by our actions, weaknesses or even our strengths; instead, He is moved with the burning passion of His own heart for us.

THE GOOD SAMARITAN [LUKE 10:25-37]

Let us now take a look at another story where we see Mercy and compassion together, explained by Jesus. In Luke chapter 10, a certain man asks Jesus: *"Who is my neighbour?"*. In response, Jesus shares the story of a Samaritan who was passing by a road and saw a wounded man:

> *33 But a certain Samaritan, as he journeyed, came where he was. And when he saw him, he had compassion. 34 So he went to [him] and bandaged his wounds, pouring on oil and wine; and he set him on his own animal, brought him to an inn, and took care of him. [Luke 10:33-34]*

This certain Samaritan had compassion for a wounded person, and in response, took certain actions. He bandaged his wounds, poured oil and wine on him, set him on his donkey, and then brought him to an inn and took care of him. These actions were done to the wounded man because of "compassion" from within the inner being of this certain Samaritan.

After Jesus finished the story, He asked:

> *36 So which of these three do you think was neighbor to him who fell among the thieves? [Luke 10:36]*

And he replied:

> *37 And he said, "He who showed Mercy on him." Then Jesus said to him, "Go and do likewise." [Luke 10:37]*

The actions that were shown to the wounded man because of compassion were acts of Mercy. Once again, we see here that Mercy is an action performed for the sake of one, because of the compassion in the heart of the one who performs it.

In these stories, the people who received Mercy were all needy and could not help themselves. They received Mercy not because they did or did not deserve, but rather, because they were in a situation whereby, they could not help themselves due to their weakness. They needed someone to have compassion for them and show them Mercy, taking them out of their problem and weakness.

Reading the beginning of the story, we find out that before the Samaritan showed up, two other people passed by the wounded man but did not help him. Jesus tells the story:

> *31 Now by chance a certain priest came down that road. And when he saw him, he passed by on the other side. 32 Likewise, a Levite, when he arrived at the place, came and looked, and passed by on the other side. [Luke 10:31-32]*

These two people were specifically a "Priest" and "Levite". The priests were always from the tribe of Levi, the tribe that was commissioned by God to be a priesthood, and to stand before God and man for the forgiveness and redemption of people. Their job was to bear the brokenness of people, to have compassion and Mercy on people. They were to do this by bringing acceptable sacrifices to God and asking God, for forgiveness and Mercy on people. They were also called to be a mediator, having the right to stand before God and intercede for people without looking at the sin of people, but instead, by having confidence in the Mercy of God. It was their duty to approach God for people, bringing His goodness in the life of the sinners.

Nevertheless, in this particular story, Jesus shows that even though that was their job, they ignored the wounded man and passed him by, without having reached out to this wounded soul to show God's goodness to him. Jesus, as a Samaritan and the One who was not of the tribe of Levi, is then called upon to be a High Priest whom, unlike the Levitical priesthood, has compassion on people and shows them Mercy. His priesthood is not according to the Levitical order, but rather, is in a different order called "Melchizedek":

> *5 So also Christ did not glorify Himself to become High Priest, but [it was] He who said to Him: "You are My Son, Today I have begotten You." 6 As [He] also says in another [place]: "You [are] a priest forever according to the order of Melchizedek". [Hebrews 5:5-6]*

The word "Melchizedek" means "king of righteousness". He is the king of a city called "Salem" which means "peace". Therefore, He is both king of righteousness and king of peace. This new order of priesthood is of righteousness and peace. Jesus, therefore, came in the new order of Melchizedek, as the king of righteousness, king of peace, and His new order changed priesthood from Levitical to Melchizedek. Due to this change, there is also a need for changing the law:

> *12 For the priesthood being changed, of necessity, there is also a change of the law. 13 For He of whom these things are spoken belongs to another tribe, from which no man has officiated at the altar. 14 For [it is] evident that our Lord arose from Judah, of which tribe Moses spoke nothing concerning priesthood. [Hebrews 7:12-14]*

And,

15 And it is yet far more evident if, in the likeness of Melchizedek, there arises another priest 16 who has come, not according to the law of a fleshly commandment, but according to the power of an endless life. 17 For He testifies: "You [are] a priest forever according to the order of Melchizedek." [Hebrews 7:15-17]

The new law, of the new order, is according to the "Power" of an "Endless Life". This means that the new priesthood is to be everlasting, with no future changes. The old order of Levites could not be everlasting because of the death of the priests. Every priest under the Levitical priesthood subsequently died and; hence, their priesthood was interrupted.

Jesus brought a new order of priesthood that will never change, because He will never die, but will live forever:

23 Also, there were many priests because they were prevented by death from continuing. 24 But He, because He continues forever, has an unchangeable priesthood. 25 Therefore He is also able to save to the uttermost those who come to God through Him since He always lives to make intercession for them. [Hebrews 7:23-25]

Unlike the Levitical priests who could not continue on forever, bringing salvation to people, as they themselves were bound to death, Jesus will not die but will live forever. As such, He can continue to forever save those who come to Him.

Jesus, as the new High Priest of the new order, established a new law. This law is the basis of righteousness and peace because He is the king of both. Therefore, His righteousness and peace toward people will never change. That is why, when Jesus told the story of the Samaritan, He pointed to the change of priesthood from Levies to another. The Levitical priesthood could never bring perfection to mankind:

11 Therefore, if perfection were through the Levitical priesthood (for under it the people received the law), what further need [was there] that another priest should rise according to the order of Melchizedek, and not be called according to the order of Aaron? [Hebrews 7:11]

The Levitical priesthood made nothing perfect. But even beyond this, despite their priesthood, they never realized the heart of God for people. They had corrupted themselves, and people, by judging and condemning people, rather than justifying them before God. It was given to them to be mediators of the covenant; to forgive and release people's sin through the offerings and sacrifices, which were acceptable to God. Not only did they not do this, they also became accusers of their own brethren, leaving the wounded behind, passing them by, and never reaching out to help them. This is why it was necessary that the old order come to an end, and a new order be established with new priests. The new priests will have a different heart, showing Mercy every single time, without any accusation or judgment against people.

When Jesus, as the Good Samaritan, sees a wounded man, He will not leave him without help. This new High Priest came to bring peace and reconciliation between man and God, as a true Mediator bringing righteous judgment to the wounded by showing them Mercy; never asking why or accusing them of having fallen short of the glory. This new order of priesthood does not look for the "why" and "what" behind the situation, but instead, shows Mercy by having compassion on the weak and needy.

> *26 For <u>such a High Priest was fitting for us</u>, [who is] <u>holy</u>, <u>harmless</u>, <u>undefiled</u>, <u>separate from sinners</u>, and has become <u>higher than the heavens</u>; 27 who does not need daily, as those high priests, to offer up sacrifices, first for His own sins and then for the people's, for this He did once for all when He offered up Himself. [Hebrews 7:26-27]*

I believe the reason that these two people, the priest and Levi, passed by the wounded man and never helped him, was because they examined and judged him in their hearts. They began to think and reason in their hearts as to "why" he had fallen into his situation. They invariably chose to "judge" him as "worthy" of his situation and then passed by him and never showed Mercy. The reason I think this, is that these are the same people who came to John the Baptist, questioning him about who he was, and why he was baptizing people:

19 Now, this is the testimony of John when the Jews sent priests and Levites from Jerusalem to ask him, "Who are you?" 20 He confessed, and did not deny, but confessed, "I am not the Christ." 21 And they asked him, "What then? Are you Elijah?" He said, "I am not." "Are you the Prophet?" And he answered, "No." [John 1:19-21]

After they did not hear what they wanted to hear, they said:

25 And they asked him, saying, "Why then do you baptize if you are not the Christ, nor Elijah, nor the Prophet?" [John 1:25]

These same people, rather than reconciling the people to God and not counting their trespasses against them, had become accusers and judges who would examine people and count their sin against them. However, according to Psalm 103, God does not count people's sin against them; rather, He has Mercy on us because He knows our weakness:

10 He has not dealt with us according to our sins, nor punished us according to our iniquities. 11 For as the heavens are high above the earth, [So] great is His Mercy toward those who fear Him; 12 As far as the east is from the west, [So] far has He removed our transgressions from us. [Psalm 103:10-12]

God had established a *priesthood* such that people may stand before God and be forgiven of their sins, have Mercy bestowed upon them, versus judgement and condemnation. For this reason, Jesus, finishing His story of the wounded man, tells us to do the same as the Samaritan and not act as an accuser, counting people's mistakes and sins against them. He shows us that we must rise up in our identity as "true priests" according to the order of Melchizedek, knowing who our High Priest is: "Merciful" and "Compassionate". As true priests of the new order initiated by Jesus, we are to hear the heart of God for those who are wounded, showing them Mercy as He would show us Mercy, because we have a sacrifice that is accepted by God: Jesus!

A MAN BORN BLIND [JOHN 9:1-4]

Jesus demonstrated the new order of priesthood in another story, teaching the disciples to be the same:

1 Now as [Jesus] passed by, He saw a man who was blind from birth. 2 And His disciples asked Him, saying, "Rabbi, who sinned, this man or his parents, that he was born blind?" [John 9:1-2]

The disciples, like the Levites and priests, were also trying to find out who had committed sin and what sin had caused such person to be in that situation. It is very likely that by finding out the reason, they would have also passed by the blind man without showing him Mercy, just as the Levites and priests in the story of the wounded man!

But Jesus, as a true High Priest, who has come according to a different order of priesthood, is not here to diagnose the problem; He is here to have compassion on the needy by showing them the work of God, His Mercy:

3 Jesus answered, "Neither this man nor his parents sinned, but that the works of God should be revealed in him." [John 9:3]

In this answer, He takes the focus off the sin and puts it on the power of God, which was about to be seen and experienced through this weakness. A priest, even as God instructed it under the old system, is not supposed to look at sinners and find fault in them, but rather, the priest is to look at the sacrifice and find Mercy for the sinners. If the sacrifice is acceptable in the sight of God, then the sins are forgiven. So, Jesus was not concerned about who or what had caused this sickness, but rather having confidence in the Mercy of God, foreseeing that the sacrifice of His own body and blood was acceptable to God, healed the blind man and showed him Mercy.

As the gospel of Matthew writes:

17 That it might be fulfilled which was spoken by Isaiah the prophet, saying: "He Himself took our infirmities and bore [our] sicknesses." [Matthew 8:17]

Mercy changes our focus from looking at man's weakness to God's strength; from our own abilities to His power; and from our sin to His righteousness. This kind of perspective freely allows us to have hope and rejoice when we are in a time of need, because we know that His power is about to be experienced in us.

Paul writes in his second letter to the Corinthians:

30 If I must boast, I will boast in the things which concern my infirmity. [2 Corinthians 11:30]

However, in the next chapter, he tells us the reason for boasting in infirmities:

9 And He said to me, "My grace is sufficient for you, for My strength is made perfect in weakness." Therefore, most gladly I will rather boast in my infirmities [weakness], that the power of Christ may rest upon me. [2 Corinthians 12:9]

Paul does not express his desire to be weak. Quite the opposite - he shows us a way out of weakness. He changes our perspective by lifting our eyes up from our own weakness, and focusing them on the power of Christ, which can be completely manifested in us! In essence, he is boasting about the power of Christ, which is made perfect in weaknesses.

Then he adds:

10 Therefore I take pleasure in infirmities [weakness], in reproaches, in needs, in persecutions, in distresses, for Christ's sake. For when I am weak, then I am strong. [2 Corinthians 12:10]

Here we see that Paul takes pleasure in the strength or power that comes in weakness, and he takes pleasure in his weakness for *"Christ's sake"*. Reading in the context, *"for Christ's sake"* refers to the power of Christ that is made perfect in weakness! Moreover, what he is also trying to say is that the weaknesses are not for us to carry along in our lives, but rather, we are to overcome them by the power of God.

As David says in his Psalm:

4 Who redeems your life from destruction, who crowns you with lovingkindness (Mercy) and tender Mercies. [Psalm 103:4]

Paul further writes:

4 For though He was crucified in weakness, yet He lives by the power of God. For we also are weak in Him, but we shall live with Him by the power of God toward you. [2 Corinthians 13:4]

Therefore, Christ has come to bring another perspective - a true perspective through which we can rejoice, even though we might experience weakness, a place where we can truly hope when everything is against such hope. Hope is where we can rise, dance, and be glad because our God has prevailed, we are not leaning on our own strength, but His strength in us. By having this kind of High Priest, who has a burning passion in His inner beings to show us Mercy, we can have the assurance of heart, that He will never leave us wounded. He is Merciful and Faithful to help us in the time of temptations and weaknesses:

17 Therefore, in all things He had to be made like [His] brethren, that He might be a Merciful and faithful High Priest in things [pertaining] to God, to make propitiation for the sins of the people. 18 For in that He Himself has suffered, being tempted, He is able to aid those who are tempted. [Hebrews 2:17-18]

He can be Merciful and Faithful because He, Himself, has gone through sufferings, and can therefore, sympathize with us, while also helping us in times of temptation. Under this new order of priesthood, because of His righteous judgments toward us, we are not to receive the consequences of our own errors that are done through ignorance. Instead, we are to be assured that He does not deal with us according to our sin, but to His Mercy instead. We can come to Him boldly, with full assurance of heart, that we will receive His Mercy whenever needed:

14 Seeing then that we have a great High Priest who has passed through the heavens, Jesus the Son of God, let us hold fast [our] confession. 15 For we do not have a High Priest who cannot sympathize with our weaknesses but was in all [points] tempted as [we are, yet] without sin. 16 Let us, therefore, come boldly to the throne of grace, that we may obtain Mercy and find grace to help in time of need. [Hebrews 4:14-16]

In this chapter, I wanted us to fully understand that compassion (the burning passion in the heart of God, our great High Priest) is the very reason why He shows us Mercy! I will be building further on this in the next Chapter when I talk more about compassion and its practicality through the Good Shepherd.

We, therefore, rejoice:

> *16 But I will sing of Your power; Yes, I will sing aloud of Your Mercy in the morning; For You have been my defense and refuge in the day of my trouble. 17 To You, O my Strength, I will sing praises; For God [is] my defense, My God of Mercy. [Psalm 59:16-17]*

Mercy, The Compassion of the Shepherd

Jesus introduces Himself as the "Good Shepherd" in the gospel of John:

> *11 I am the good shepherd. The good shepherd gives His life for the sheep. [John 10:11]*

With respect to those who came before Him, Jesus says:

> *8 All who [ever] came before Me are thieves and robbers, but the sheep did not hear them. [John 10:8]*

Here, He makes a strong statement that those who came before Jesus and called to be shepherds and leaders of His people were nothing more than thieves and robbers! We further read in verse 10:

> *10 The thief does not come except to steal, and to kill, and to destroy. I have come that they may have life and that they may have [it] more abundantly. [John 10:10]*

Jesus refers to the shepherds and leaders who came before Him as thieves and robbers, because they did not care for and safeguard the sheep. Rather, they stole, killed, and destroyed the sheep.

But Jesus says of Himself, *"I have come that they may have life"*. The previous shepherds did not give life to the sheep, the Good Shepherd calls them "thieves".

God had defined the shepherd's responsibility as that of taking care of the sheep and feeding them, just as we read in Ezekiel 34:

> *2 Son of man, prophesy against the shepherds of Israel, prophesy and say to them, thus says the Lord GOD to the shepherds: Woe to the shepherds of Israel who feed themselves! Should not the shepherds feed the flocks? 3 You eat the fat and clothe yourselves with the wool; you slaughter the fatlings, [but] you do not feed the flock. 4 The weak you have not strengthened, nor have you healed those who were sick, nor bound up the broken, nor brought back what was driven away, nor sought what was lost, but with force and cruelty, you have ruled them. 5 So they were scattered because [there was] no shepherd, and they became food for all the beasts of the field when they were scattered. [Ezekiel 34:2-5]*

The shepherds were supposed to feed the sheep, strengthen the weak, heal the sick, bind up the broken, bring back the ones who were scattered and go to the lost sheep and restore them. Not only had they not cared about the sheep, but their lack of caring for the sheep also resulted in the sheep becoming scattered and falling prey for the beasts to devour them.

A few verses later we then read:

> *10 Thus says the Lord GOD: "Behold, I [am] against the shepherds, and I will require My flock at their hand; I will cause them to cease feeding the sheep, and the shepherds shall feed themselves no more; for I will deliver My flock from their mouths, that they may no longer be food for them." [Ezekiel 34:10]*

We read in verse 5 that the sheep became food for the beasts: *"...they became food for all the beasts of the field"*, but later in verse 10, Ezekiel says that they are food in the mouth of their own shepherds: *"...the shepherds shall feed themselves no more; for I will deliver My flock from their mouths"*. If we connect these two scriptures together and read them in the context, we realize that the "beast" which devours the sheep must be the "mouth" of these "false shepherds". Rather than feeding and caring for the sheep, the shepherds instead made food for themselves by slaughtering the sheep and feeding themselves. This is why Jesus indicates that all the shepherds who came before Him were thieves and robbers. They came only to steal, kill and destroy His sheep by feeding themselves. However, in these verses the Lord also says that He will get the sheep out of their mouth and deliver them; His sheep will no longer be food for the false shepherds. It is for this reason that Jesus says: *"I am the good shepherd"*, because He, as a shepherd, has not come to slaughter the sheep to give life to Himself, but rather, to give Himself to the mouths of the beasts so that His sheep can flee out from their mouths and live.

This is clearly illustrated on the night that Jesus was betrayed, arrested and delivered to be crucified. After they had finished the last supper, they went to Mount Olive and Jesus spoke to them:

> *31 Then Jesus said to them, "All of you will be made to stumble because of Me this night, for it is written: I will strike the Shepherd, And the sheep of the flock will be scattered." [Matthew 26:31]*

Jesus, the one who was to be crucified, is the Good Shepherd who would lay down His life for His sheep so that His sheep could flee from the mouths of the beasts, scatter and be saved. It is for this reason that He willingly stepped forward and offered Himself to the soldiers when they arrived at where He was:

> *7 Then He asked them again, "Whom are you seeking?" And they said, "Jesus of Nazareth." 8 Jesus answered, "I have told you that I am [He]. Therefore, <u>if you seek Me, let these go their way.</u>" [John 18:7-8]*

Jesus is the Good Shepherd for He does not give His sheep to the mouths of the beasts, but rather, He takes His sheep out of the mouths of the beasts and places Himself in their mouths to save His sheep. This illustrates Jesus' willingness to taste "death", so that we may have "life" and have it more abundantly!

If we continue reading Ezekiel 34, we realize that it is the Lord Himself who will seek the sheep and feed them:

11 For thus says the Lord GOD: "Indeed I Myself will search for My sheep and seek them out." [Ezekiel 34:11]

And then,

14 "I will feed them in good pasture, and their fold shall be on the high mountains of Israel. There they shall lie down in a good fold and feed in rich pasture on the mountains of Israel. 15 I will feed My flock, and I will make them lie down." says the Lord GOD. [Ezekiel 34:14-15]

Due to the fact that no one was able to properly care for the flock of the Lord, He Himself had to come and tend to His sheep by being the Good Shepherd and doing what everyone else before Him had failed to do. First, He gave Himself to the mouths of the wild beasts and tasted death. Then He rose again, as the ever-living Good Shepherd, to forever lead and feed His flock in "green pastures".

In multiple places in the Bible we read, including Psalm 23 that says the Shepherd leads the sheep to "green pastures" and "still waters" where they can eat and drink and take rest:

1 A Psalm of David. The LORD [is] my shepherd; I shall not want. 2 He makes me to lie down in green pastures; He leads me beside the still waters. [Psalm 23:1-2]

Next, let us better understand how it is that the Good Shepherd leads and "feeds" His flock. If Jesus is the Good Shepherd, we need to understand what our "food" is.

36 But when He saw the multitudes, He was moved with compassion for them, because they were weary and scattered, like sheep having no shepherd. [Matthew 9:36]

The gospel of Mark adds even more detail to this by saying:

34 And Jesus, when He came out, saw a great multitude and was moved with compassion for them because they were like sheep not having a shepherd. So, He began to teach them many things. [Mark 6:34]

Jesus had "compassion" for people, therefore, He began to "teach" them many things. Compassion arose in His heart because He saw that His people were like sheep that were going astray in the absence of a shepherd. These scriptures clearly illustrate to us that the "feeding" of the sheep is the "teaching" that the Good Shepherd provides to them, which we have also come to know provides us "Life".

It is the Good Shepherd's "compassion" for His sheep that causes Him to take action and "feed" the sheep with His own life. In the absence of the Good Shepard, the sheep lacked "Good Food"; it is His "Good Food" that are the "teachings" that provide life, not death, to us. It is the lack of teaching of life that causes us, as His sheep, to suffer hunger, look for food in other places and become devoured by the wild beasts and die.

As our Good Shepherd, Jesus teaches us and feeds us good food because He has compassion for us. He does not want us to be scattered and later die. Rather, He wants us to be gathered to Him and to have life in abundance. He feeds us by teaching us about the life (of the Spirit), which is His act of Mercy toward us.

The False Shepherds, mentioned by Ezekiel and Jesus, did not feed the sheep by giving them good teachings so that the sheep could live. Instead, they devoured the sheep by false doctrine and caused the sheep to die. Not only did all those who came before Jesus not teach about food that would give life, but they also caused the sheep to eat foods that would instead bring death.

In the third chapter of Genesis[7], Adam and Eve ate of the fruit of a tree called the "Tree of Knowledge of Good and Evil". In doing so, "death" was brought to them. Adam and Eve had unwittingly fallen "prey" into the mouth of the "serpent" by having mistakenly accepted a false "knowledge" that the serpent had deceptively offered to them. It was a "knowledge" that Adam and Eve did not need to have. The

---

[7] Genesis 3:1-11

"knowledge" given to them by the serpent became a "food" that they ate and was a "food" which would later cause them to die.

What we are to learn from this is that what causes mankind to "die", generation after generation, is mankind's mistaken acceptance of a "knowledge" that is false, not needed or otherwise simply not good for us. We can also call these "teachings".

Whenever someone hears knowledge, that person has the opportunity to believe it, think about it, speak it and act upon it - thus producing either life or death. "False shepherds" are the ones who bring the kinds of teachings to mankind (referred to as the "doctrine of man" or the "wisdom of the world") that have been inherited from the serpent and cause the sheep (mankind), to die. But Jesus said:

> *11 I am the good shepherd. The good shepherd gives His life for the sheep. 12 But a hireling, [he who is] not the shepherd, one who does not own the sheep, sees the wolf coming and leaves the sheep and flees; and the wolf catches the sheep and scatters them. 13 The hireling flees because he is a hireling and does not care about the sheep. 14 I am the good shepherd, and I know My [sheep] and am known by My own. 15 As the Father knows Me, even so, I know the Father; and I lay down My life for the sheep. [John 10:11-15]*

Jesus came, not to flee from the wolves, but rather to give Himself to the wolves for the freedom of His sheep. If the mouths of the wolves illustrate the doctrine and teachings of the False Shepherd, then it is here that we can see Jesus handing Himself over to the leaders of the law to be crucified, according to their doctrine.

Those who were determined to crucify Jesus went to Pontius Pilate saying:

> *7 The Jews answered him, "We have a law, and according to our law He ought to die because He made Himself the Son of God." [John 19:7]*

They always had a reason, a doctrine or a law that they could use to sentence someone to death. Their teaching never produced life and never gave life to anyone. They placed burdens on people's shoulders; heavy burdens that were difficult for people to carry and burdens which they themselves would not help the people carry, even with one of their fingers[8]. They had the keys to open the heavenly doors, but they shut the doors of the kingdom of heaven instead. They themselves did not go in and neither did they let anyone else enter in[9]. They had closed the way to life by bringing false doctrines to the people; this was never the doctrine of God. In doing so, they caused His sheep to scatter and wander without life-giving food to eat.

When Jesus began His ministry by teaching in every synagogue, people were amazed at His teachings saying:

> *22 And they were astonished at His teaching, for He taught them as one having authority, and not as the scribes. [Mark 1:22]*

And,

> *32 And they were astonished at His teaching, for His word was with authority. [Luke 4:32]*

His teachings were with authority, with power, and with life. That is why when we read in Luke chapter 4, Jesus while teaching in the synagogue, heals a demon-possessed man:

> *33 Now in the synagogue, there was a man who had a spirit of an unclean demon. And he cried out with a loud voice, 34 saying, "Let [us] alone! What have we to do with You, Jesus of Nazareth? Did You come to destroy us? I know who You are, the Holy One of God!" 35 But Jesus rebuked him, saying, "Be quiet, and come out of him!" And when the demon had thrown him in [their] midst, it came out of him and did not hurt him. 36 Then they were all amazed and spoke among themselves, saying, "What a word this [is]! For with authority and power, He commands the unclean spirits, and they come out." [Luke 4:33-36]*

Jesus' words were life-giving and His teachings were powerful and with authority. People were drawn to Him for they had never experienced anyone like Him. Thousands left their jobs and began to follow Him daily because they had found something that they had

---

[8] Matthew 23:4
[9] Matthew 23:13

never seen in any of their own leaders. The sheep had finally found their own Good Shepherd. They were finally being fed with food and had life. At His words, the storm, the wind, and the seas were calm. Blind eyes could see, the deaf could hear, the lame could walk, and the dead rose came back to life.

By giving up His life for the sheep, Jesus prepared good food for the sheep to eat and live. Here we see that this "food" is a "teaching" and that this teaching must be related to Him giving Himself to the mouth of wolves. Through this teaching, the sheep learn that when the wolf comes, it is the Good Shepherd who will go forward to be the food for the sheep and thus they will be saved. The teachings that give life to the sheep are a "doctrine" about His death. The death of Jesus teaches us, as His sheep, to eat and drink from Him, and in doing so, have life.

In John 6 Jesus speaks of the food that comes from His death. It is His body, broken for us; and His blood, which was shed on the cross:

> *51 I am the living bread which came down from heaven. If anyone eats of this bread, he will live forever; and the bread that I shall give is My flesh, which I shall give for the life of the world. [John 6:51]*

And,

> *53 Then Jesus said to them, "Most assuredly, I say to you, unless you eat the flesh of the Son of Man and drink His blood, you have no life in you. 54 Whoever eats My flesh and drinks My blood has eternal life, and I will raise him up at the last day. 55 For My flesh is food indeed, and My blood is drink indeed. 56 He who eats My flesh and drinks My blood abides in Me, and I in him." [John 6:53-56]*

And,

> *58 This is the bread which came down from heaven- not as your fathers ate the manna and are dead. He who eats this bread will live forever. [John 6:58]*

Jesus, as the Good Shepherd leads His sheep to "green pastures" and "still waters" where they can eat and drink "good food" and have life eternal. This good food is His flesh (the green pasture) and His blood (the still waters); it is provided to His sheep at His death on the cross. Jesus leads His sheep to the cross, where He died to teach them about His death so that the souls of His sheep can be restored, through eating His good food and having life everlasting, as prophesied in Psalm 23:

> *1 A Psalm of David. The LORD [is] my shepherd; I shall not want. 2 He makes me to lie down in green pastures; He leads me beside the still waters. 3 He restores my soul; He leads me in the paths of righteousness for His name's sake. [Psalm 23:1-3]*

End of this Psalm the Psalmist says:

> *6 Surely goodness and Mercy shall follow me All the days of my life, and I will dwell in the house of the Lord forever. [Psalm 23:6]*

I mentioned earlier in this chapter that Jesus saw the crowd and was moved with compassion for them because they were like sheep without a shepherd, so He began to teach them. These sheep without a shepherd were scattered and would later die. However, His compassion for the sheep moved Him to provide teachings to the sheep that would cause them to gather, eat of the good food and therefore live. Since the teaching of the Good Shepherd is an action that was done because of the compassion of His heart, it is, therefore, the Mercy of God.

The Mercy of God comes to the picture when God sees that we, like sheep, are being scattered, wandering around and not knowing where we are going. When our soul is thirsty, tired and in lack of peace, He comes to find us and lead us back to a place where our soul is at rest; a place where we are gathered to Him, settled in heart, filled with His food and therefore at peace. He, as the Good Shepherd, leads us to an understanding of His body and blood. Understanding what He has done for us through His body and blood brings us rest from our labour.

The Good Shepherd wants us to live and not die. He wants us to live a life that is filled with abundance of His peace, joy, rest and life. Therefore, He extends His Mercy to us by giving us good food, leading us to green pasture where we can lay down, rest, eat and not be afraid even in the presence of our enemies.

In the past we were scattered, hurt, and were dying not because of anything we had done, but because of not having a Good Shepherd to take care of us. We had to fight with the wolves of wilderness and run for our lives. We struggled to find food and longed for a drink of water to quench our thirst. A sheep does not have legs to run like a deer; it does not have the ability to attack or defend itself from the wolves; nor does it have an ability to look and hunt for food. Undoubtedly, sheep are the only living-souls that must rely fully on their shepherd for life. Therefore, because we did not have a Good Shepherd, we became a prey to the wolves.

But now that we have come to the Good Shepherd, who is the lover of our soul, we can be in the presence of our enemies and never fear! We can have this assurance that our Good Shepherd does not run away when the trouble comes to us, but rather, He is the one who comes to our aid, protecting us and causing the wolves to cease from our dwelling place; He brings restoration to our soul thereby causing us to live.

In the book of Revelation, John the apostle records a vision that he was shown about a group of people led by the Lamb to the still waters. This Lamb is their Good Shepherd:

> *17 For the Lamb who is in the midst of the throne will shepherd them and lead them to living fountains of waters. And God will wipe away every tear from their eyes. [Revelation 7:17]*

We read a similar account in chapter 21 with some more details:

> *4 And God will wipe away every tear from their eyes; there shall be no more death, nor sorrow, nor crying. There shall be no more pain, for the former things have passed away. [Revelation 21:4]*

Verse four reads: *"God will wipe away every tear from their eye"*, and then adds: *"there shall be no more death, nor sorrow, nor crying, nor pain"*. Then we read the reason: *"the former things have passed away"*. The "former things" were tears, death, sorrow, crying, and pain. When the "former things" pass away, we are free from all that is in the "former things".

We further read in chapter 7 that God will wipe away every tear from their eyes when the Lamb shepherds the flock to the fountain of the living water. Putting these two scriptures together we realize that the fountain of the living water is where the "former things" no longer exist anymore. That is why we can come to drink from this fountain and rest.

Next, let us better understand what this fountain of the living water actually is.

Chapter seven of the gospel of John records an account of Jesus in the last day of the last feast of the year in Jewish tradition, called the "Feast of Tabernacle", as follows:

> *37 On the last day, that great [day] of the feast, Jesus stood and cried out, saying, "If anyone thirsts, let him come to Me and drink. 38 He who believes in Me, as the Scripture has said, out of his heart will flow rivers of living water." [John 7:37-38]*

Then the next verse explains what this river of living water is:

> *39 But this He spoke concerning the Spirit, whom those believing in Him would receive; for the Holy Spirit was not yet [given], because Jesus was not yet glorified. [John 7:39]*

The Lamb, who is the Shepherd, leads the sheep to the "living waters". This living water is the Holy Spirit and is given to those who believe in Jesus. In the Spirit, all "former things" are washed (pass) away. Verse 37 tells us that this Spirit "flows" forth like a river of water from those who come to Spirit to eat and drink.

Earlier in this Chapter, I mentioned that, through His death, eating and drinking from Him gives us life. While it is through these teachings concerning His flesh and blood that we are fed by Him, Jesus Himself also teaches us that life does not come from flesh itself, but rather, from the Spirit:

> *63 It is the Spirit who gives life; the flesh profits nothing. The words that I speak to you are spirit, and [they] are life. [John 6:63]*

Are these teachings somehow in contradiction with one another? The answer is 'no'. Here Jesus is telling us two things. Firstly, that the Spirit-given revelation of His flesh and blood "gives" us life. Secondly, that the eating of His flesh and blood must be done through the revelation and understanding that the Spirit gives to us, and then it will "be" life. In other words, the river of living water is the Spirit that constantly reveals His flesh and blood to us. When we eat and drink through the revelation of the Spirit, all former things begin to pass away and we enter into His rest and have life in abundance!

We should also reflect on the truth that this living water flows out of us. It is not external to us, it dwells within us. The Spirit comes to live on the inside of us when we are believers, it can also flow back out from within us.

Therefore, the Lamb that shepherds us to eat of green pasture and drink of living waters lives inside of us! The One who died on that cross - the crucified Christ; the Lamb - dwells inside of us. He tasted death for every individual, thus He is individually in every one of us. We do not need to look for food somewhere out there. The food we need is not far from us - it is in our heart. We do not need to go up to heaven to bring it down, nor to the depths of the sea to bring it up. It is already here within us; in our heart and in our mouth[10].

This Good Shepherd leads us into the deep places of our own beings where He Himself resides. He tells us what He has done for us so that we can have "a knowledge" and "a teaching", but this time it is a kind that brings us life, not death. His death is in us which means death has happened once for us, thus the former things, which had death in it for us, must pass away. It was appointed for every man to die once and because Christ has died for everyone and He is inside of every believer, death cannot happen twice to that person. In other words, His life (the flow of the Spirit), comes out from the darkest and

[10] Romans 10:6-8

deepest places of man's heart, flowing like a river, thus watering the dry land of the body, bringing to life the dead places and making it a fruitful land once again: The Garden of Pleasure (Eden) of the Lord.

Jesus speaks of the water of life, once more, in the gospel of John. Let us now look at this story.

Jesus met a Samaritan woman who had come to a well of water, which Jacob had given to his sons. Jesus asked the woman to give Him a drink of water. The woman was hesitant to do so because Jews did not have anything to do with a Samaritan, but this Jew was different:

> *10 Jesus answered and said to her, "If you knew the gift of God, and who it is who says to you, 'Give Me a drink,' you would have asked Him, and He would have given you living water." [John 4:10]*

And,

> *11 The woman said to Him, "Sir, You have nothing to draw with, and the well [pit] is deep. Where then do You get that living water? 12 Are You greater than our father Jacob, who gave us the well, and drank from it himself, as well as his sons and his livestock?" [John 4:11-12]*

The woman explains to Jesus that all her ancestors came to this well (the correct translation is "pit") and would draw water from it using a bucket. Therefore, she must use a bucket to draw water from the deep well.

Jesus tells her that if she drinks of this kind of water she will thirst again; she will have to come again to draw more and will find herself labouring more, to have more, in order to quench her thirst and yet never be satisfied.

Jesus tells this story to illustrate that what the woman was doing symbolizes the stage in life of those who are "dry and thirsty" in their soul, whom labour and toil to quench the thirst of their soul in whichever way they can think of. In doing so, will be to no avail because it will become a never-ending cycle that will never quench the thirst of one's soul.

Instead, we see that Jesus introduced a different kind of water. A kind of water that she did not need to labour for because there was no need for her to go down to a pit to draw it out. Rather, this kind of water flows upwards from the pit, like a spring (fountain) of water and releases one from labour, and hence, from thirst!

> *13 Jesus answered and said to her, "Whoever drinks of this water will thirst again, 14 but whoever drinks of the water that I shall give him will never thirst. But the water that I shall give him will become in him a fountain of water springing up into everlasting life." [John 4:13-14]*

Sometimes I can feel the excitement in the heart of this woman when she heard these things, saying:

> *15 The woman said to Him, "Sir, give me this water, that I may not thirst, nor come here to draw." [John 4:15]*

What she was hearing was already giving her rest in her soul, a resounding hope to be free from the labour and curse, which had entered the world since her forefathers. Now here was this Man offering her something that could set her free from the way of living, which was inherited by her from her forefathers!

Then Jesus, in response to her request, told her to call her husband and come back. She replied by telling Jesus that she did not have a husband. Later, Jesus reveals that she had lived with five men in the past and that the one she was living with was not her husband. I believe that what caused her to labour to quench the thirst of her soul and necessitated her having to come to a pit and try to draw water, was the lack of a husband. The man she was living with was not a husband to her, which is why she had come to get the water by herself. The man did not help her, nor did he do anything to lift a burden off her shoulder. Jesus however, as a "True Husband" of the "Bride", stands in front of her and symbolically represents His church by saying to her:

"I will give you a kind of water that you do not need to labour for, a kind of water that will give you rest and you will never thirst again".

He also said that this water will be like a fountain, springing up from the well unto eternal life:

> *14 But whoever drinks of the water that I shall give him will never thirst. But the water that I shall give him will become in him a fountain of water springing up into everlasting life. [John 4:14]*

We saw in the book of Revelation that it is the Good Shepherd that leads the sheep to the fountain of the living water. Therefore, the Good Shepherd is also the True Husband who gives His bride freely whatever she asks. In this particular case, it is the fountain of the living water that quenches her thirst, releases from her labour and brings rest to her soul because a covenant now exists between them: a covenant of peace!

This covenant of peace is placed between the Husband and the Bride; the Good Shepherd and the Sheep. The Good Shepherd who comes to bring the covenant of peace comes according to the Sure Mercies of David, as Ezekiel says in chapter 34:

> *22 Therefore I will save My flock, and they shall no longer be a prey, and I will judge between sheep and sheep. 23 I will establish <u>one shepherd</u> over them, and he shall feed them- <u>My servant David</u>. He shall feed them and be their shepherd. 24 And I, the LORD, will be their God, and My servant David a prince among them; I, the LORD, have spoken. 25 I will make <u>a covenant of peace</u> with them, and <u>cause wild beasts to cease from the land</u>, and they will dwell safely in the wilderness and sleep in the woods. [Ezekiel 34:22-25]*

In these verses, the Lord tells us that David will be a shepherd over His people. However, we know that He is not speaking of king David himself, as this prophecy of Ezekiel came years after David was gathered to his forefather. Rather, this is a prophecy about the one who was going to come from the loins of David, according to the flesh. Thus, the true shepherd who would deliver the flock from death and feed the flock with life is Jesus, the Christ, who received the Sure Mercies of David according to Acts chapter 13.

33 God has fulfilled this for us their children, in that He has raised up Jesus. As it is also written in the second Psalm: "You are My Son, Today I have begotten You." 34 And that He raised Him from the dead, no more to return to corruption, He has spoken thus: "I will give you the Sure Mercies of David." [Act 13:33-34]

Christ, the one who is now raised from the dead is the one that was referred to as David in order to point at the Sure Mercies of David. The resurrection of Jesus from the dead means that He shall be returned to corruption no more! Therefore, because His resurrection has already happened, we can then say that this Mercy is Sure! That is why He is now able to give us this Mercy and we can have the assurance of it!

Reading Ezekiel, we again see that this Good Shepherd will show Mercy to the sheep by strengthening the weak, healing the sick, bounding up the broken, feeding the sheep, and delivering them from death and causing the wild beast to cease from the land:

25 I will make a covenant of peace with them and cause wild beasts to cease from the land, and they will dwell safely in the wilderness and sleep in the woods. [Ezekiel 34:25]

Not only does He feed the sheep with good food and deliver the sheep from the wolves, but He also causes the wolves (the wild beasts) to cease from the land because He has a covenant of peace with the sheep.

His peace comes to the sheep when their land is free of any wild beasts that might cause trouble for the sheep. When the land is cleansed of the beasts, the sheep can dwell safely in the land and sleep in the green pasture, with no fear of any trouble or attacks.

Thus, it is David who brings the covenant of peace through the Sure Mercies. This David, who is the Christ, is the leader and the shepherd. It is because of Him that there is to be peace for the sheep. Therefore, the covenant of peace is established because of the Mercy of the Good Shepherd.

Isaiah the prophet writes:

10 "For the mountains shall depart and the hills be removed, But My kindness shall not depart from you, nor shall My covenant of peace be removed," Says the LORD, who has Mercy on you. [Isaiah 54:10]

His covenant of peace cannot be removed because He has Mercy on us. This Mercy endures forever!

The true shepherd is not a hireling. The hireling shepherds who came before Jesus did not show Mercy to the sheep and that is why the sheep were scattered and experienced death.

The problem has never been about how weak we, the sheep, are, but rather, the lack of a Good Shepherd. Nevertheless, now we have come to the Shepherd of our soul:

25 For you were like sheep going astray but have now returned to the Shepherd and Overseer of your souls. [1 Peter 2:25]

Jesus showed throughout the gospels, directly or indirectly, that He is the Good Shepherd. He has come for the sheep, having compassion on us, not judging or criticizing the weakness of our flesh, but rather, sympathizing with us.

We read in the gospel of Matthew:

14 And when Jesus went out He saw a great multitude; and He was moved with compassion for them and healed their sick. [Matthew 14:14]

But in the next verse His disciples come to him, saying:

15 When it was evening, His disciples came to Him, saying, "This is a deserted place, and the hour is already late. Send the multitudes away, that they may go into the villages and buy themselves food." [Matthew 14:15]

The disciples told Jesus to send the crowd away so that they would go find food for themselves! But it was for this exact reason He came, to feed the sheep. How could He now send them away to go and gather food for themselves?

It is for this reason that Jesus answers:

16 But Jesus said to them, "They do not need to go away. You give them something to eat." [Matthew 14:16]

Throughout the generations, the sheep sought food for themselves because there was no shepherd to give them food. In doing so, as we have previously learned, the sheep were devoured by the wild beasts of wilderness. Now that Good Shepherd has come, we see that He will not send them away but, instead, will feed them.

Jesus tells His disciples to feed the people, showing that all of His followers are shepherds and must feed the flock of God. Peter later understood this and wrote:

2 Shepherd the flock of God which is among you, serving as overseers, not by compulsion but willingly, not for dishonest gain but eagerly; 3 nor as being lords over those entrusted to you, but being examples to the flock; 4 and when the Chief Shepherd appears, you will receive the crown of glory that does not fade away. [1 Peter 5:2-4]

At the time, however, neither Peter nor any of the other disciples recognized that they were supposed to feed the flock, as a shepherd. Instead they, like others, reasoned why the sheep could not be fed:

17 And they said to Him, "We have here only five loaves and two fish." [Matthew 14:17]

And the gospel of John records the same story and adds:

9 There is a lad here who has five barley loaves and two small fish, <u>but what are they among so many</u>? [John 6:9]

They had a reason, which so many of us may have as well: "It is not possible to feed five thousand people with only five loaves of bread and two small fish".

But Jesus did not have such reasons. He knew "all things are possible to those who believe". He obviously had another reason! Instead, He took the five loaves and two small fishes, blessed them and fed the five thousand people. He did something that they thought they could not do. He showed them that it was possible. Jesus, knowing that

He had come as the Good Shepherd with the Sure Mercies of David, did not send the flock away to find food for themselves on their own. Rather, He instead fed them because His Mercy is sure! I believe because of the assurance of God's Mercy, He was convinced that it was possible to feed the crowd because His Mercy is everlasting. I believe the reason the disciples wanted to send the people away and thought they could not feed the crowd was that they did not yet know His Mercy! They did not know yet His Sure Mercy for themselves or for the people. In fact, they immediately wanted to do the same thing that their forefathers had done over the years. They could not show Mercy to the flock and would cause the flock to be scattered because they, themselves, had never received His Mercy.

In the scripture below, Peter tells us the good news of our redemption from the useless and fruitless way of living that we inherited from our forefathers. I like the amplified version of this verse:

> *18 For you must know (recognize) that you were redeemed (ransomed) from the useless (fruitless) way of living inherited by tradition from [your] forefathers, not with corruptible things [such as] silver or gold, but [you were purchased] with the precious blood of Christ (the Messiah), like that of a [sacrificial] Lamb without blemish or spot. [1 Peter 1:18 AMP]*

One of the things mankind has been inheriting from their forefathers for many generations is: "not knowing His Mercy"! They did not feed the flock thinking, "this is not possible". The reason one thinks, "this is not possible" is simply because one does not know or believe His Sure Mercy.

Jesus' reasoning, at all times, was different than the disciples. His kind of reasoning caused Him to do what He did, making the impossible, become possible. The reasoning of the disciples was "it is not possible because no one has done this!". Yet Jesus did things that the disciples, like many of us, thought were impossible. He showed the impossible is possible if we just believe in His Mercy. Mercy causes all things to become possible. Mercy has life within itself. When it comes, it surpasses all situations, bringing with it blessings, multiplication and the abundant life.

It is the job of Mercy to intervene when there is a lack and by triumphing over it, show us a new way of living and leading us unto eternal life:

> *21 Keep yourselves in the love of God, looking for the Mercy of our Lord Jesus Christ unto eternal life. [Jude 1:21]*

Mercy, The Only Reasoning

In the previous chapter, we concluded that Mercy is what makes all things possible because Mercy shows up when there exists a lack, weakness or impossibility. Mercy provides a solution that goes beyond the current natural arguments, and therefore, makes possible what seems to be impossible.

Jesus in the ninth chapter of the gospel of Mark says:

> *23 Jesus said to him, "If you can believe, all things [are] possible to him who believes." [Mark 9:23]*

However, before He makes this strong authoritative statement, we see a story through which Jesus reveals what it is that must be believed, in order to do the impossible.

Jesus, after coming down from the mount transfiguration, finds His disciples disputing with scribes and teachers of the law. He then asks for the reason for their dispute:

> *16 And He asked the scribes, "What are you discussing with them?" 17 Then one of the crowd answered and said, "Teacher, I brought You my son, who has a mute spirit. 18 And wherever it seizes him, it throws him down; he foams at the mouth, gnashes his teeth, and becomes rigid. So, I spoke to Your disciples, that they should cast it out, but they could not." [Mark 9:16-18]*

There was a boy who needed healing. His father brought him to the disciples but they could not heal his boy. Therefore, the father told Jesus:

> *22 And often he has thrown him both into the fire and into the water to destroy him. But if You can do anything, have compassion on us and help us. [Mark 9:22]*

It was right after this that Jesus said:

> *23 Jesus said to him, "If you can believe, all things [are] possible to him who believes." [Mark 9:23]*

The father asked for help from Jesus because he had brought his son to the disciples and they could not heal him. He knew that the help he had asked for comes from a compassion which was not found in the disciples, because they had instead gotten into dispute and discussion with the teachers and leaders of the law, rather than healing the boy by having compassion on the sick. When the father saw compassion in Jesus, he knew that if Jesus could have compassion on his son, He could also help the father by healing his son.

The same story is told in Matthew 17 but in more detail. We read that the father of the boy came to Jesus and asked Him to have Mercy on his son:

> *14 And when they had come to the multitude, a man came to Him, kneeling down to Him and saying, 15 "Lord, have Mercy on my son, for he is an epileptic and suffers severely; for he often falls into the fire and often into the water. 16 So I brought him to Your disciples, but they could not cure him." [Matthew 17:14-16]*

The boy's father asked Jesus for help which was the Mercy that he needed in that situation. It was then that Jesus told the father, *"If you can believe, all things [are] possible to him who believes"*. The impossible was about to happen because of the Mercy that Jesus was going to show. For this reason, Jesus told the father to continue believing in His Mercy and all things will be possible.

Mercy is designed to make the impossible, possible because Mercy comes out of the compassionate heart of God. The compassion in His heart moves Him to take action. In turn, it is His action that brings help to us and removes our burdens from us.

When no one and nothing is able to help, Mercy can! For this reason, Mercy must be our only argument and reasoning in answering this question: "Why must the impossible happen?".

When we believe in God's Mercy, *"with God"*, all things are and will be possible. If we look closer, we see that that scripture says, *"with God"* and not, *"for God"*. This tells us that the impossible is made possible through "cooperation" between man and God. Man, alone, is not capable of making all things possible. But God, on the other hand, made man in His own image and likeness to reign on earth over all the works of His hand. While it is man's "job" to do that, doing so is only possible through man's belief in God. Therefore, in this so-called "cooperative with God", man's part is to believe God; God's part is to perform the truth that man believes about God.

Since God is the everlasting, ever remaining, powerful almighty creator, and besides Him, there is no other god, then man can believe that God can and will do the impossible. He can make the "impossible", "possible". I think this is truly amazing and comforting!

Looking at the story of the father with the sick boy, the disciples got into a dispute with the teachers of the law instead of "believing". As we learned earlier above, the dispute resulted in their inability to heal the boy. Their reasoning was not in accordance with Mercy, but rather, it fueled "faithless" dispute over matters of the law. After Jesus heard what had happened, He said to them:

> *17 Then Jesus answered and said, "O faithless and perverse generation, how long shall I be with you? How long shall I bear with you? Bring him here to Me." [Matthew 17:17]*

I believe that Jesus did not say, *"O faithless and perverse generation"* to the father, nor to the boy, nor the scribes, and the Pharisees. He said this to the disciples who had gotten into the argument. Even though this statement could also be pointed at the scribes, Pharisees, and any others who were present there with Him at the time, it was His disciples who were with Him all the time, seeing His Mercy and miracles. It was His disciples who were commanded, ordained, and given authority to go heal the sick! Yet now they had fallen into a trap that generation after generation of their fathers before them had fallen into, foolish arguments!

We need to see the loving heart of Jesus in this story and not perceive Jesus as having been frustrated. Generation after generation of people who were "predestined" to be conformed to the image of God and who were to walk as Sons of God in power, authority, and dominion over the evil of sickness and death, have been falling into the same foolish arguments. This pattern has held man back from walking in the fullness of God on earth.

Let us now look at some scriptures to find out what Jesus meant by "faithless and perverse generation".

The word used for "perverse" in Greek is "diastrephō" which means, "turning one aside from a path or a direction". This word is used in Acts 13, as follows:

> *6 Now when they had gone through the island to Paphos, they found a certain sorcerer, a false prophet, a Jew whose name [was] Bar-Jesus, 7 who was with the proconsul, Sergius Paulus, an intelligent man. This man called for Barnabas and Saul and sought to hear the word of God. 8 But Elymas the sorcerer (for so his name is translated) withstood them, seeking to turn [to pervert] the proconsul away from the faith. [Acts 13:6-8]*

The proconsul was interested in hearing the word of God, but a false prophet who was a Jew withstood Saul and the message that He was preaching, in order to turn the proconsul away from faith! "To turn away" in this verse is "to pervert". He was trying to pervert and turn the proconsul away from the way of faith! The manner in which he did this is also clear. He did so by bringing about disputes, arguments and false knowledge. He was a false prophet and also a Jew.

Since Saul, who had become Paul, was preaching about the justification "by faith", not justification "by the works of the law", the false prophet withstood Paul because he was a Jew and believed in the justification "by works of the law of Moses"! From this, we learn that messages that pervert the true message of faith are messages that still rely on the works of the law and not justification by faith in Jesus Christ.

The story continues:

> *9 Then Saul, who also [is called] Paul, filled with the Holy Spirit, looked intently at him 10 and said, "O full of all deceit and all fraud, [you] son of the devil, [you] enemy of all righteousness, will you not cease perverting the straight ways of the Lord?" [Acts 13:9-10]*

Paul's statement in these verses provides a clearer understanding of the word "perverse". According to Paul, the way of "faith" is the "straightway of the Lord". But by contrast, "perversion" turns away from faith. In other words, according to scripture, a "perverse" person is someone who has turned away from faith.

Looking back at the story of the father with his son, we can now better understand why the disciples were not able to heal the boy. They were "perverted" from the "straightway of the Lord" which is "faith" and "believing"; they had fallen back into the works of the law, entrapped within, by the arguments and debates they were having with the teachers of the law, concerning the matters of the law.

It appears that when the father brought the boy to the disciples to be healed, the teachers of the law appeared, bringing with them arguments concerning the law that clouded the minds of the disciples, causing them to be drawn into an argument with the teachers. By doing this, the disciples had turned themselves away from faith and the boy remained sick and unhealed.

Jesus, however, healed the boy! This caused the disciples to come to Him privately afterwards and ask Him why they could not do it:

19 Then the disciples came to Jesus privately and said, "Why could we not cast it out?" 20 So Jesus said to them, "Because of your unbelief; for assuredly, I say to you, if you have faith as a mustard seed, you will say to this mountain, 'Move from here to there,' and it will move, and nothing will be impossible for you." [Matthew 17:19-20]

Jesus' answer to the disciples was clear, "because of your unbelief"! The reason they could not cast the demon out of the boy was "unbelief".

The disciples were commissioned earlier to go and preach the gospel, heal the sick, and cast out demons everywhere, which they did. But somehow, they could not heal that boy.

The reason the father of the boy brought him to the disciples was because of previous experiences of them healing the sick. People were bringing their sick to them, just as they did to Jesus! But in this particular story, the teachers of the law showed up with their "reasoning" and caused the disciples to turn away from the simplicity of the gospel: "if you can believe".

Perhaps the teachers' "legalistic" reasoning seemed worth considering to the disciples, but in doing so, they forgot that it was His compassion that releases Sure Mercy, and Sure Mercy is the only reason behind the healing of the sick.

Therefore, "the faithless and perverse" generation is one that turns from the straightway of the Lord, which is faith, and instead, falls into the law. It is a generation that does not believe that "*with God all things are possible*". It is a generation that does not believe that *"if you believe, all things are possible for those who believe"*, but instead, thinks that there must be something done in order to receive something in return from God. But the father of the boy understood this. He came to Jesus and put his hope in His Mercy, believing that if He could just have compassion on him, then he could receive the sure Mercy promised by God to the fathers.

Here is what we read about "unbelief":

> *23 Jesus said to him, "If you can believe, all things [are] possible to him who believes." [Mark 9:23]*

In desperate need of healing, the father answered:

> *24 Immediately the father of the child cried out and said with tears, "Lord, I believe; help my unbelief!" [Mark 9:24]*

He wanted to believe and he actually did believe which is why when the disciples could not heal his son, he did not give up and ran to Jesus next to heal his son. Due to his initial "reasoning", he began wavering, not really knowing if he had any faith. He then cried out to Jesus to help him in overcoming his "unbelief"! Yet in the midst of all of the confusion, arguments, debates, and offences surrounding them, Jesus was still able to heal the boy!

I am not sure about you, but when I read stories like this, I want to know what caused Jesus to be able to heal that boy while the disciples could not. What was going on in His mind? What different thoughts was He having? What was He seeing and understanding that we do not? I need to know the answer to these questions because I believe that we are called to be conformed to His image[11] - to think like Him, to see like Him, to talk like Him, and even act like Him. It is my belief that this is what we all need to grow into. I also believe that the answer to the questions is that Jesus knew who He was "The Son of God!". He knew He was the Son of the Father. This is something that we are still discovering. We must grow both into the fullness of Him and into the level of maturity that He purposed us to be in.

At one time, we as mankind lived like orphans do, without God, and without a Father. As His lost children, God found us and brought us to His own house. Even though we became the children of the family of God, we are children who are still growing into the likeness and fullness of Him. Our approach is sometimes not from the mind of a "Son" of God, instead, we may still find ourselves thinking and talking like an orphan about things we must do to save ourselves, while the truth says we are the "sons" of our Father. This is why the book of

---

[11] Romans 8:29

Deuteronomy talks about the "perverse generation" (the generation that does not live by "faith" in God), as those who had forgotten that they are the children of God and He is their Father:

> *5 They have corrupted themselves; [They are] not His children, Because of their blemish: a perverse and crooked generation. 6 Do you thus deal with the LORD, O foolish and unwise people? [Is] He, not your Father, [who] bought you? Has He not made you and established you? [Deuteronomy 32:5-6]*

These forgetful children are those who "corrupt themselves". They have forgotten that the God, who brought them out of slavery and protected them along the way, is a Father who takes care of His children. By forgetting the truth about themselves, they have corrupted themselves, and have become a perverse generation, having no faith.

Remembering who we are as His children, and that God is our Father, produces faith within us. By knowing the Father, we know that He is compassionate and Merciful toward His children. Thus, we also believe in His Mercy. Just as Jesus said to the father of the boy, once we believe *"in Him"*, then *"with Him"*, all things are possible. This father also had compassion for his own son but was too weak to bring him help, so he instead brought his son to another Father who also has compassion on His own children. This Father, God, makes all things possible because of the compassion of His heart, which is greater than the weakness of His children's carnal flesh.

Since we are children of God, and we know that God is our Father, we can and should believe in His Mercy in every situation. We are not of those who do not have hope and are weak when faced with adversity and challenges. Quite the opposite! We are strong for He is "in us and with us". Even though we may not yet have grown up into a fully matured Son of God, we believe in our Father and we trust in His Mercy towards the maturity. When we express complaints and doubts, we are forgetting this truth. But when we steadfastly believe that He is compassionate towards us and shows us Mercy, there is no reason to complain or have doubts.

Paul, in Philippians 2, encourages all of us as children of God to be blameless, harmless, and without fault in the midst of the crooked and "perverse generation", so that we can shine in the darkness:

> *15 That you may become blameless and harmless, children of God without fault in the midst of a crooked and perverse generation, among whom you shine as lights in the world. [Philippians 2:15]*

The verse that comes before that, tells us what it means to be harmless and blameless in the midst of the perverse generation:

> *14 Do all things without complaining and disputing. [Philippians 2:14]*

Children of God are to do all things "without complaining and grumbling". Doing so makes them "blameless, harmless, and without fault" in the midst of the crooked and perverse generation.

The perverse generation is a generation that complains and grumbles when doing things. Even though they are His children, they have forgotten that God is their Father. Complaining and grumbling is a sign that there is no faith in His Mercy and as the result, miracles do not happen. Mercy does not manifest and healing does not happen, just as we have seen in the story of the disciples who could not heal the boy.

The perverse generation is a generation that does not believe in God's Mercy. For this reason, when things happen in this kind of generation, the generation only sees their own limitlessness and powerlessness, rather than the hand of God as Father in their lives. In the absence of hope and belief, this generation is left instead to grumble and complain. But the amazing part is that in the middle of this crooked generation, God's Mercy never fails, once someone is turned towards Him! His Mercy is never taken away from anyone. Over and over again He comes to rescue His own children and bring them out of the darkness and corruption that they have made for themselves. We see that in the story of the Israelites, as Nehemiah says:

15 You gave them bread from heaven for their hunger and brought them water out of the rock for their thirst and told them to go in to possess the land which You had sworn to give them. 16 But they and our fathers acted proudly, hardened their necks, and did not heed Your commandments. 17 They refused to obey, and they were not mindful of Your wonders that You did among them. But they hardened their necks, and in their rebellion, they appointed a leader to return to their bondage. <u>But You [are] God</u>, <u>Ready to pardon</u>, <u>Gracious and Merciful</u>, <u>slow to anger</u>, <u>abundant in kindness</u>, and did not forsake them. [Nehemiah 9:15-17]

Also, we read in Psalm 106:44-45:

44 Nevertheless, He regarded their affliction when He heard their cry; 45 And for their sake He remembered His covenant and relented according to the multitude of His Mercies. [Psalm 106:44-45]

We truly are the children of God, not only in words but also in action. We are the straightway of the Lord, the way of faith. Why should we corrupt ourselves by speaking words like those who do not have a Father? Our heart's desire is to shine as a light and enlighten the heart of others. If we find ourselves missing this point, we are to hang onto His Mercy and believe that His Mercy is not limited to the mistakes we make.

When the children of Israel complained, many died by the serpents. Others lived, however, despite being bitten by the serpent, simply because they realized that they had missed the mark by the way of their tongue:

7 Therefore the people came to Moses, and said, "We have sinned, for we have spoken against the LORD and against you; <u>pray to the LORD that He take away the serpents from us.</u>" So, Moses prayed for the people. [Numbers 21:7]

Therefore,

8 Then the LORD said to Moses, "Make a fiery [serpent], and set it on a pole; and it shall be that everyone who is bitten when he looks at it, shall live." 9 So Moses made a bronze serpent, and put it on a pole;

and so, it was, if a serpent had bitten anyone when he looked at the bronze serpent, he lived. [Numbers 21:8-9]

Many are bitten by the serpent, daily and repeatedly, and unfortunately, many die without ever having realized that there is another way out: HIS MERCY!

This Mercy comes through the compassionate heart of God in order to give life to those who are bitten by the serpent, by way of their own tongue! If we acknowledge His compassionate heart and believe in His Mercy, we will not suffer from our mistakes. Rather, we will receive what He died for. Mercy is able to make a way out of sin, corruption, weakness, and death. Mercy brings redemption and life.

God demonstrated His Mercy to the children of Israel by instructing Moses to lift up a serpent on a pole, so that people could continue living just by looking at the serpent. This was a foreshadowing of the redemption that was to come through Jesus. If we can look upon Him on the cross, we can continue to live and not die:

14 And as Moses lifted up the serpent in the wilderness, even so, must the Son of Man be lifted up, 15 that whoever believes in Him should not perish but have eternal life. [John 3:14-15]

Even though many, like the children of Israel, are bitten by the serpent because they have opened their mouths to complain, grumble, and corrupt themselves by way of their tongues, the end does not need to be death. We can lift up our eyes and look at the One who is on the cross and realize that He took upon Himself what had bitten us. He drew the sting out of us, causing us to live, thus receiving His Mercy.

Mercy needs to be the way we think, the way we reason, and the way we live. Otherwise, we continue to be victims of our fleshly imperfection.

Most of us have heard sayings such as, "nobody is perfect!" or "to err is human!". However, even though this has been the reality of man since the first man, Adam, Jesus came to deliver us from the limited life of Adam. He came to put His Spirit in us, to empower us, and to teach us a better way of living, which Adam and all those who have come from the loin of Adam have missed. This has been missed because the "Adamic" nature is easily drawn to reasoning, feelings, and things that can be seen and touched. The more humanity is engaging in the Adamic nature, the further humanity is from believing in the power of God, and relying on His Mercy.

Jesus offers a new way of living that comes through His new way of thinking. Our aim in life should be to live a life with the Spirit of God, or in other words, fire the old teacher and start listening to, and learning from, the new one. Our "old teacher" taught us many things according to past experiences and we were trained to rely on our own thoughts and ourselves! This is the reason we fall into foolish arguments and fail. Our fears "ground" us, even though we were made to fly; it is because of our fears that we never use our wings.

If we desire to experience a better life, a life that Jesus introduces, we need to start by changing the way we "think and reason" within ourselves.

If we continue to think like the old, we will live like the old. But if we allow ourselves to see what He put in front of our eyes to see - "why He did what He did" - then we begin to realize a new way of living, His way of living! A place where we realize that He made us for freedom, to be free from fear by lifting our eyes up to the sky, opening our wings and letting the wind of the Spirit to take us up. This is how we are to live with Him, flying through Him and with Him.

Mankind has failed many times in the past, the fear of failure and rejection dominates humanity. Most of us, over time, have built a cage around ourselves, and by doing so have lost the ability to trust others. But ironically, the one that we should not trust is ourself because the only one who has failed us is us! We should, therefore, be bold and dare to trust one other: God, Himself. For it is He alone who is forever compassionate toward us. Even though He might tell us to jump, He is certain that He will catch us. It is He who has done all things to convince us that He is worth believing. He is what we want. He is what we need. He is what we desire. He is our life, our hope, our destiny, the purpose of our creation and our reward!

It might be that we have been introduced to Him incorrectly and so we run away from Him or feel that we cannot easily trust Him. But if we push past our fear and draw closer to know Him, we can discover who He really truly is. He will change the way we think and open our eyes to the life of co-working with Him where "all things will be possible".

It only starts when we decide to change the way we think. For all of us, it can start here and it can start now!

Mercy, A Help in the Storm

Many of us have gone through challenges in life, times that we often refer to as the "storms of life". In those times our souls were not at rest, we were anxious, worried and fearful, not knowing what would happen next.

Some of us have even suffered a loss in those storms, such that we have lost our peace and live in the fear of tomorrow's "potential" storms, even though we are not necessarily experiencing or going through a storm in the here and now.

In this chapter, we will discover that the ultimate plan of God for us is to live a life where storms have no power and authority over us. This can only be achieved when we allow Him to teach us how (and believe) we can rely on His attributes to help us survive and overcome the storms of life. This has been God's plan since the creation of man, that man become mature and grow up to a "Perfect Man", a true "Son of God", who is not ruled by the storms, but rather, holds dominance over such storms.

Mercy, as one of the most powerful attributes of God, will come to our aid when we are caught in a storm where there is no hope. His Mercy comes to us to lift us up, protect us and empower us not only to pass through the storms with no loss but also to give us a rest with no fear of tomorrow's storms because His Mercy is always available to help us to overcome!

The writer of the book of Hebrews writes in the 4th chapter:

> *16 Let us, therefore, come boldly to the throne of grace, that we may obtain Mercy and find grace to help in time of need. [Hebrews 4:16]*

The Greek word used for "Help" in this verse, is found only in one more place in the New Testament, which is in Acts 27, but translated as "cables":

> *17 When they had taken it on board, they used cables to undergird the ship; and fearing lest they should run aground on the Syrtis [Sands], they struck sail and so were driven. [Acts 27:17]*

This chapter of the book of Acts, tells the story of Paul the apostle who was going to Rome to testify about Jesus. As a prisoner with other prisoners, he got on a boat to go to Rome. Paul perceived that this voyage would end with much loss and disaster, so he warned others not to sail, but they decided instead to sail once they saw the wind begin to blow softly. Soon after, however, a tempestuous head wind arose and they were trapped within the tempest for many days:

> *20 Now when neither sun nor stars appeared for many days, and no small tempest beat on [us], all hope that we would be saved was finally given up. [Acts 27:20]*

Before giving up hope, they did everything they could do to save the ship and its sails. We read in verse 17 that they used cables to "undergird" the ship to "help" binding the ship together. The word "undergird", is a combination of two words: "Under" and "Gird", and it means: "to bind a ship together with girths or cables, to enable it to survive the force of waves and tempest[12]". Basically, in the time of waves, tempest, or storm they bind the ship with cables so that the storm and the tempest will not crush the ship into pieces, helping the ship to survive until the storm is finished!

---

[12] Definition is taken from Strong's Concordance G5269

By comparing this verse with Hebrews 4:16 we can see what the "Cable" is. The word "Cable" used in verse 17 is the same word that is translated as "Help" in Hebrews 4:16, which is used to "undergird" a ship in tempest:

> *16 Let us, therefore, come boldly to the throne of grace, that we may obtain Mercy and find grace to help [cable] in time of need. [Hebrew 4:16]*

So, the writer of the book of Hebrews likens God's Mercy and grace to "cables" that can be used in the time of need. Mercy, like these cables, can undergird a ship to hold the ship together in the time of storm and tempest, so that the ship can endure and survive until the tempest is gone. Mercy and grace are sought after when we are in a time of need. According to these scriptures, the time of need for Mercy and grace is when "storms" come. Therefore, Mercy holds us and binds us together in our times of need, so that we can endure the storms. We will see shortly what the storms and waves are. However, before proceeding any further, we first need to understand more about the symbolism of a "ship" that is caught in a storm and in need of help.

There is another combination of the word "gird" (zōnnymi) with the word "up" (ana) that together form the word "anazōnnymi", which means, "to gird up". This word is used in the first epistle of Peter:

> *13 Therefore gird up [anazōnnymi] the loins of your mind, be sober, and rest [your] hope fully upon the grace that is to be brought to you at the revelation of Jesus Christ. [1 Peter 1:13]*

Here we see that Peter likens the mind to a loin and indicates that just as a loin needs to be tightened up by a girdle, the mind also must be girded up. The mind must not fall apart; it should remain joined, focused and determined.

A girdle is used to cinch and hold something together. In the disciples' time, a girdle was used to bind a money bag so that treasures or money could be placed and carried inside of it, where it would be protected.

Similarly, our mind is a place where we keep our "treasures" or, in other words, our "thoughts". When we want the treasures in our minds to remain safeguarded and not lost, we "gird" our mind to keep the treasures in place. Our minds hold and process millions of thoughts daily. These thoughts are treasures and must be held cohesively together; otherwise, they can run amuck or go astray in multiple directions.

Our mind becomes "sober" when it is "girded up". In other words, when we are sober in mind, we can be steadfast in faith and in our belief in God. Being in this particular state of mind fosters our ability to more easily resist the temptations that come through the adversary, as Peter writes at the end of his epistle:

> *8 Be sober, be vigilant; because your adversary the devil walks about like a roaring lion, seeking whom he may devour. 9 Resist him, steadfast in the faith, knowing that the same sufferings are experienced by your brotherhood in the world. [1 Peter 5:8-9]*

We learn that the "mind" is like a "ship" and needs to be girded up with the "cables" of Mercy. These so-called cables of Mercy hold our thoughts together so that they do not go astray when we encounter the winds and storms of life. It is Mercy that helps us to remain focused, sober, alert, and hopeful. It enables us to forge on in faith when we are in the midst of adversity and difficulty (the "wilderness" times) in our life. God's Mercy helps us endure these hard times - the "winds and storms" of life - without experiencing loss or ruin.

Let us now next look at the "waves and winds".

James writes to the brethren in Christ, that we should be rejoicing when we face trials. The word "trial" in this verse is "temptation". This means that when we encounter temptation, we should rejoice for the following reason:

> *2 My brethren, count it all joy when you fall into various trials [temptation], 3 knowing that the testing of your faith produces patience. 4 But let patience have [its] perfect work, that you may be perfect and complete, lacking nothing. [James 1:2-4]*

But he then adds:

> *5 If any of you lacks wisdom, let him ask of God, who gives to all liberally and without reproach, and it will be given to him. 6 But let him ask in faith, with no doubting, for he who doubts is like a wave of the sea driven and tossed by the wind. [James 1:5-6]*

The one who "doubts" is likened to the "waves" of the sea. These waves are created, driven, and tossed by the "wind". To understand the symbolism of the "wind" we can look at Ephesians 4:

> *14 That we should no longer be children, tossed to and fro and carried about with every wind of doctrine, by the trickery of men, in the cunning craftiness of deceitful plotting. [Ephesians 4:14]*

Here we see that a "wind" represents a "doctrine". Just as a wind causes waves to be tossed around in multiple directions, a doctrine causes people to be tossed to and fro. This doctrine is of man and not God. When instead of one direction we find ourselves in various directions, we can find ourselves in doubt. In other words, the "wind" of doctrine causes the "waves" of doubts to rise up in one's mind. This shows us that the thoughts of the mind move like a ship in every direction, tossed to and fro by the waves of doubt when it is driven by various doctrines.

People whose lives are represented by this analogy are called "children" in Ephesians 4:14. We are not called to remain as "children", but we are called to be mature "sons". Children are not grown up, nor are they mature. Maturity is "the fullness of the stature of Christ". Those who are mature in Christ have grown to the "Unity of Faith" and they cannot be easily forced into the tempest waves of doubt. Children, however, can get caught up in the storm and tossed around, instead of being stable in what is to be believed. The wind of doctrine, which causes doubts to rise up in people, is a teaching that originates from man. Its "craftiness" tricks people by deceiving them and leading them away from the truth, instead of towards it. This doctrine does not allow children to grow and mature; when these winds followed, those following such winds will not experience the maturity and the fullness of Christ.

The word "craftiness" is used five times in the New Testament. Therefore, understanding the significance of the word "craftiness" will help us understand the way the doctrine of man operates. Paul uses this word to connect the story of first deception by the serpent to the today's deceptions in the church:

> *3 But I fear, lest somehow, as the serpent deceived Eve by his craftiness, so your minds may be corrupted from the simplicity that is in Christ. [2 Corinthians 11:3]*

It was the serpent that corrupted Eve's mind by her craftiness. It is the "craftiness" that came through the serpent that has become the "doctrine of man". The story of the Garden of Eden is where Paul gets his analogy. By reading the story, we realize that all the serpent did was to bring about "another" idea, "another" suggestion, and "another" voice to contradict the word that God had originally spoken. That "second" idea, "second" suggestion and "second" voice became a teaching, a doctrine that corrupted her mind from the simplicity of God's word. Eve's mind was no longer stable, with a single option, but was deceived; it had received corruption, and hence, death entered the world.

God had simply told them not to eat of the fruit of the knowledge of good and evil lest they would die:

> *16 And the LORD God commanded the man, saying, "Of every tree of the garden you may freely eat; 17 but of the tree of the knowledge of good and evil you shall not eat, for in the day that you eat of it you shall surely die." [Genesis 2:16-17]*

But serpent came along with another idea: "You will not surely die":

> *4 Then the serpent said to the woman, "You will not surely die. 5 For God knows that in the day you eat of it your eyes will be opened, and you will be like God, knowing good and evil." [Genesis 3:4-5]*

The simplicity of the word of God was now twisted in the mind of Eve and she was deceived, so she instead ate what was to bring death to her! However, before she ate of the fruit, she first had a thought, that it was "good":

> *6 So when the woman saw that the tree [was] good for food, that it [was] pleasant to the eyes, and a tree desirable to make [one] wise, she took of its fruit and ate. She also gave to her husband with her, and he ate. [Genesis 3:6]*

As pointed out previously, Eve did not eat the evil, but rather, she ate the good! In her mind, she thought that the fruit was good and would benefit her, but this very reasoning brought death to her. Adam, and everyone else who came in the likeness of Adam, all have had the same pattern of thoughts. They have reasoned the same, and therefore, have all died in like manner! That is why Paul says that there is "simplicity" in the gospel, but the "craftiness" that came from serpent brings with it confusion, complication, and eventually deception. This simplicity (which literally means "singleness") was replaced by duality because of "other" doctrines. In other words, the mind of man experiences corruption through other suggestions that is apart from the word of God.

The doctrines of man were inherited from the serpent, they corrupt the mind of man. The corruption is brought about by doubts that go through man's mind. The mind is then caught in a storm and its thoughts are driven in every direction. If Mercy is not received and is not used to gird up the mind, these times of doubts will cause the ship (the mind) to be tossed about in multiple directions. Overcome and overburdened by doubts, the mind sinks down and does not reach its intended "destination", rather, it suffers confusion and loss!

But what is this so-called "destination"? It is what we are intended to grow into, "Christ". We were predestined to a destination called the "Perfect Man", which is the "Stature of the Fullness of Christ" as revealed by Paul in Ephesian 4.

Before proceeding any further, let us look first at what Paul writes about the word "craftiness" in his first letter to Corinthians:

> *19 For the wisdom of this world is foolishness with God. For it is written, "He catches the wise in their [own] craftiness". [1 Corinthians 3:19]*

It was man who brought this "craftiness" into the world or, in other words, a wisdom that looked "good" when in fact it was foolishness - just as Eve looked at the fruit of the tree of the Knowledge of Good and Evil and saw it as "good"; something that could make her wise. Therefore, the "wisdom" that seemed "good" entered the world through one man, but it was foolishness to God because it brought death. We should pay closer attention to the fact that this doctrine which brings death also carries with it wisdom. This is why many are enticed to take it and are then deceived. They receive the wisdom thinking it is good, thus feeding on it. But it is the "wisdom of the world". This kind of wisdom is crafty and comes through the serpent to corrupt the simplicity of the word of God. Worldly wisdom is contrary to the wisdom of God; it causes a tempest to arise, the mind to struggle with doubts and brings with it loss which, in the end, is death.

The period of time in which "doctrine and wisdom of man" come deceptively and persuasively to us is called "the time of temptation" in James chapter 1. It is when mankind hears (and listens to) a wisdom or doctrine that is contrary to the doctrine of Christ and His wisdom. By doing so, mankind falls prey to "worldly" promptings and temptations, rather than following the Spirit of God.

In Luke chapter 20 some spies came to Jesus asking a question to test and "tempt" Him, but Jesus discerned their "craftiness":

> *20 So they watched [Him], and sent spies who pretended to be righteous, that they might seize on His words, in order to deliver Him to the power and the authority of the governor. 21 Then they asked Him, saying, "Teacher, we know that You say and teach rightly, and You do not show personal favouritism, but teach the way of God in truth: 22 Is it lawful for us to pay taxes to Caesar or not?" 23 But He*

perceived their craftiness, and said to them, "Why do you test[13] [tempt] Me?" [Luke 20:20-23]

Jesus perceived their craftiness, the wisdom of the serpent, which came through man to cause temptation. Therefore, the wisdom of man comes to bring temptation against the wisdom of God, which is His word.

The gospels record the account of Jesus in the wilderness. He was led into the wilderness to be tempted by the devil for forty days. After the time of temptation was over, the devil left him for an opportune time[14]. From that time onward, we do not see devil coming to tempt Jesus. But demons and unclean spirits were constantly manifesting in His presence, through people falling down at His feet and crying out that He was the Son of God. However, these were "people" who came to test and "tempt" Him. They, by their "craftiness" received from the serpent and through the fall of man, had become serpents, broods of the serpent, doing what their fathers did before them - testing and "tempting" God.

When temptation comes, it carries wisdom alongside of it. This wisdom is of the serpent, worked out through man, and our entire world operates under it. It is the doctrine of man - an advice or even a voice that has come in contrary to the truth we have known and believed. What enables us to overcome the wisdom of the serpent is the wisdom of God. Therefore, James exhorts us to ask for wisdom in the time of temptation. That is why Ephesians 4 says that "perfection" (maturity) of the church is when it is no longer like children and no longer tossed to and fro with the doctrine of man that comes from the wisdom of the world.

"Perfection" is arriving at our destination, the unity of the faith, the knowledge of the Son of God, the Christ:

13 Till we all come to the unity of the faith and of the knowledge of the Son of God, to a perfect man, to the measure of the stature of the

---

[13] Strong G3985, a verb, which means "tempt"

[14] Luke 4:13

fullness of Christ; 14 that we should no longer be children, tossed to and fro and carried about with every wind of doctrine, by the trickery of men, in the cunning craftiness of deceitful plotting. [Ephesians 4:13-14]

Wisdom establishes man. Wisdom causes man to be immovable and fully stable; standing on the word of God and believing Him in all things. The man that is built up in this way is the "Perfect Man". No man can establish himself, but God. That is why Peter, in his first epistle, says it is the God of grace who is able to establish us:

10 But may the God of all grace, who called us to His eternal glory by Christ Jesus, after you have suffered a while, perfect, establish, strengthen, and settle [you]. [1 Peter 5:10]

This God of grace is the one who sits on the throne of grace. We can boldly come to this throne of grace to receive Mercy and find grace to help us in times of need: "the time of temptations"; "the time of doubts"; and "the times the storm arises".

Until the children are grown up into this "Perfect Man", they will experience times of temptation. It is for this reason that God is available to aid them so that they would not be driven in every direction. But rather, by receiving His Mercy they would gird up the loins of their mind, stay sober, have a hope of salvation and endure to the end thereby overcoming temptation and never experiencing any loss, thus moving toward their destination- Perfection.

18 For in that He Himself has suffered, being tempted, He is able to aid those who are tempted. [Hebrews 2:18]

He helps us when we are being tempted by the wisdom of the world. This help is His Mercy that comes from His grace to gird our minds, thereby holding our thoughts together to continue believing in what we have heard from Him. Mercy helps us to overcome temptations. Grace establishes us after we come out of times of temptation and stabilizes us so that we are "immovable". Through this, we are strengthened and established in the truth of God!

25 Now to Him who is able to establish you according to my gospel and the preaching of Jesus Christ, according to the revelation of the mystery kept secret since the world began 26 but now made manifest, and by the prophetic Scriptures made known to all nations, according to the commandment of the everlasting God, for obedience to the faith. [Romans 16:25-26]

DISCIPLES IN STORM WITH JESUS [MARK 4:35-41]

The gospel of Mark gives us a short story of the disciples who got into a boat with Jesus to go to the other side of a lake. On the way a great windstorm arose, tempest waves swept into the boat and the boat began filling with water. The story is as follow:

35 On the same day, when evening had come, He said to them, "Let us cross over to the other side." 36 Now when they had left the multitude, they took Him along in the boat as He was. And other little boats were also with Him. 37 And a great windstorm arose, and the waves beat into the boat so that it was already filling. 38 But He was in the stern, asleep on a pillow. And they awoke Him and said to Him, "Teacher, do You not care that we are perishing?" 39 Then He arose and rebuked the wind, and said to the sea, "peace, be still!" And the wind ceased and there was a great calm. 40 But He said to them, "Why are you so fearful? How [is it] that you have no faith?" 41 And they feared exceedingly, and said to one another, "Who can this be, that even the wind and the sea obey Him!" [Mark 4:35-41]

While the storm rose up and the high waves began filling the boat with water, Jesus was sleeping in the "stern". The disciples raised Him up saying to him: *"Teacher, do You not care that we are perishing?"*. The disciples' reaction during the storm on the lake shows us that the boat was in a very bad situation. Most of these people were fishermen. They had been in many storms before, they knew all types of storms and if they concluded that they were perishing, it is conceivable that they were possibly drowning. Nonetheless, they had forgotten what Jesus had told them before they had gotten into the boat: *"Let us cross over to the other side"*. The Jesus who had told them to go to the other side was the one who had also said:

31 Heaven and earth will pass away, but My words will by no means pass away. [Mark 13:31]

If Jesus told them *"Let us cross over to the other side"* before they even got into the boat, or even before there was any storm, the storm was not able to change what Jesus had said! However, disciples were now experiencing something contrary to what Jesus had said.

Now in the midst of storm, they had to decide to either believe what Jesus had told them, *"we are going to the other side"*, or to believe what the storm was saying to them: "you are not going to make it to the other side of the lake; you are going to drown and perish". Doubting Jesus' words, they began to believe the storm's voice and thought to themselves: "we are going to perish". Terrified by the thought of drowning, they woke Jesus up. After the disciples awakened Jesus, He got up, rebuked the wind and said to it: "*Peace, be still*". Suddenly, the wind ceased and there was a great calm.

It is at this point that we need to understand what this story is meant to illustrate to us. If the "wind" is the "doctrine of man", a wisdom against the wisdom of God and His word, then the "waves" of the sea are intended to illustrate "doubts" that arise in our mind. The doubts begin to cause us distress and our souls are overcome with feelings of fear and torment. By rebuking the wind, Jesus "rebukes" the doctrine of man. When Jesus then speaks "peace" to the waves, he is speaking peace to man's troubled mind so that his soul is no longer in fear, but rather, remains hopeful and at peace.

After the winds had ceased, Jesus then said to those who were with Him in the same boat:

40 But He said to them, "Why are you so fearful? How [is it] that you have no faith?" [Mark 4:40]

The doctrine, teaching and wisdom of man impart fear because they are in contrary to the doctrine of Jesus which gives peace. The doctrine of man agitates the mind, distresses the heart and torments the soul, while His word brings peace. Therefore, in the midst of doubts arisen by the winds, when our souls are troubled, we can still believe in the hope of getting to the other side, passing through the storm and getting where He has said our soul is headed to: Salvation!

Had the disciples believed the words of Jesus and not what the storm was telling them, they could have rested and fallen asleep, where Jesus was sleeping, instead of being in fear and agitation. Regardless of what they were feeling, the words of Jesus would have been fulfilled and they would have arrived on the other side of the lake, just as Jesus had said they would!

Disciples In Storm Without Jesus [Mark 6:45-52]

There is also another story of a storm recorded in the gospels. This time Jesus sent His disciples to go to the other side of a lake; but in this particular story, He Himself departed from them to go to the mountain to pray:

> *45 Immediately He made His disciples get into the boat and go before Him to the other side, to Bethsaida, while He sent the multitude away. 46 And when He had sent them away, He departed to the mountain to pray. [Mark 6:45-46]*

Unlike the first story, this time Jesus was not with them in the boat but He, from the mountain, saw them struggling on the sea and He came to them:

> *47 Now when evening came, the boat was in the middle of the sea; and He [was] alone on the land. 48 Then He saw them <u>straining</u> at rowing, for the wind was against them. Now about the fourth watch of the night, He came to them, walking on the sea, and would have passed them by. [Mark 6:47-48]*

The Greek word used for "straining" also means "torment". This word is used in the gospels when someone was "tormented" by an evil spirit! In this story, the disciples were being "tormented" as they were being driven by the "wind" which was moving against them. As soon as Jesus saw them, He came to them by walking on the disturbed sea in the midst of the "waves". Upon seeing this, the disciples were terrified as they thought that they had seen a ghost!

> *49 And when they saw Him walking on the sea, they supposed it was a ghost, and cried out; 50 for they all saw Him and were troubled. But immediately He talked with them and said to them, "Be of good cheer! It is I; do not be afraid." [Mark 6:49-50]*

Once they heard His voice in midst of the wind and the waves, they recognized Him and brought Him onto their boat:

> *51 Then He went up into the boat to them, and the wind ceased. And they were greatly amazed in themselves beyond measure and marveled. [Mark 6:51]*

In this second story, similar to the first one, Jesus told His disciples to go before Him to the other side because He wanted to meet them there. Because He was not in the boat with them in this second story, He instead came to them in the midst of the storm. Because they had gotten into trouble on the water, Jesus showed up halfway through their trip on the way to the other side where they were to meet Him. Here we see that He met the disciples in the storm when they were experiencing trouble trying to make it over to the other side on their own to meet Him.

But the word of Jesus must come to pass as He, Himself, has said:

> *31 Heaven and earth will pass away, but My words will by no means pass away. [Mark 13:31]*

With this said, it is important to understand that in accordance to His word as spoken to the disciples, the fulfillment of His word was not to meet them in the middle on their way, but rather, to meet them on the other side of the lake where they were headed. John's gospel records the same story but in it, John adds more details to clarify what had happened when Jesus came into their boat:

> *21 Then they willingly received Him into the boat, and immediately the boat was at the land where they were going. [John 6:21]*

The moment Jesus got into the boat and met the disciples, they were "immediately" on land at the other side where they were headed to! With this, we are to see that even though Jesus had to come and meet them halfway through their journey, He still (in effect) met them on the other side just as He had foretold and, through this, His word was made true and was fulfilled.

When Jesus was walking on the water toward them, the disciples were frightened at first so Jesus immediately talked to them:

> *50 For they all saw Him and were troubled. But immediately He talked with them and said to them, "Be of good cheer! It is I; do not be afraid." [Mark 6:50]*

In essence, what Jesus told them was more or less like this: "Be of good cheer because I have come to you". He had come to "save" them and deliver them from the "torment" of the "wind" and "waves" of the sea! If you are in need of help along the way to fulfill what He has said to you, He will show up in the midst of your doubts, or the storm of your life to bring salvation for you and fulfill His word in your life.

In the first story, the disciples were in the storm with Jesus being in the boat with them. Even If they would not have woken Him up, they still would have arrived at the other side safely because His word will never fail. In the second story, despite a miracle being needed, the disciples immediately reached their destination in the boat and, through this, His word was again fulfilled. Jesus walked on the waves of waters which were stirred up and pretended that He was passing them by. But when He realized that they saw Him, He called to them and the disciples recognized Him. It was then that they received him into their boat and there was a great calm.

This story reveals a truth that Jesus walks on the doubts that arise in our minds. Doubts rise simply by hearing another voice, the doctrine of man or the wisdom of the world – anything that is contrary to the truth, the word of God or a prophetic word He has given us. Such voices come against what God has told us before there becomes any kind of storm in our lives. When Jesus sees us in torment, under these doubts, He comes to us; walking on our doubts and waiting for us to first acknowledge Him, then willfully receive Him into our boat. He does not force Himself on anyone, but rather, is a very present help in every storm and will get into the boat to bring a great calm whenever He is received willingly by man. When we acknowledge Him, He calls us and then we can hear His voice. The disciples heard a voice that was known to them, a voice that was full of hope: *"be of good cheer, it is I"*. It is to say "be of good cheer, I am here to help". This voice came to them in the midst of all other voices, all other thoughts and all other doubts. He came in the midst of all their fear and His voice brought hope and comfort to those of them who were tormented by the wind. And it was when they willingly received Him into the boat that there came a great calm!

The gospel of Mark ends the story by adding a few more words revealing why they ended up in this storm:

> *51 Then He went up into the boat to them, and the wind ceased and they were greatly amazed in themselves beyond measure and marvelled. 52 For they had not understood about the loaves, because their heart was hardened. [Mark 6:51-52]*

Here is the reason: *"they had not understood about the loaves because their heart was hardened".* This speaks of what had happened to them before they got into the boat and onto the water.

Just as Paul tells us in Galatians 4, concerning the two covenants symbolized by two women, the stories we read in the Bible are illustrations through which we receive wisdom. Paul further tells Timothy that all such stories become scriptures in our hand and, in reading them, we become wise for the salvation through faith that is in Christ Jesus[15]. Having said this, we need the help of the Spirit of God while we read these stories so that we may hear Him and receive from Him the revelation of what is written.

Now looking at this story in the gospel of Mark, the writer writes by the inspiration of the Holy Spirit, pointing to something that can help us understand the message:

---

[15] 2 Timothy 3:15

52 For they had not understood about the loaves, because their heart was hardened. [Mark 6:52]

This particular story took place after Jesus had fed the crowd with only five loaves. They all ate and afterwards still picked up 12 more baskets with the left-overs. The disciples entered the boat right after this occasion, but did not understand what had happened in the multiplying of the bread; possibly they were thinking or talking amongst themselves about how five thousand people could be fed with only five loaves. They may also have had arguments and discussions amongst themselves, in an effort to find some sort of explanation or "reason" for what they had just witnessed. However, as we have come to see, such efforts invariably lead them into a place of even more confusion and doubt. Their lack of understanding brought about a storm of "other voices" within themselves. Such voices are contrary to God and are what caused them distress and torment - fueled by the tempestuous storm, arising from their thoughts and reasoning. The storm they were caught in was, in effect, a manifestation of the storm that was going on inside of them. When Jesus saw them in their struggle while on the mountain, knowing they had not understood the multiplying of the bread, He again came to them!

As soon as they got out of the boat Jesus began teaching them about the bread of life because what caused them to be caught in the storm of doubts was the lack of understanding concerning the multiplying of the bread. We read this in John chapter six where He taught the crowd about the true bread of life that had come down on earth and that the multiplication of this bread in one's life is what really gives life and causes one's salvation to draw near.

The loaves that Jesus multiplied, which the disciples did not understand, was a sign of the true bread of life, which multiplies to feed as many as are hungry. The doctrine of man and the wisdom of the world which came like a wind were, however, against this bread of life and its teaching which says "if we eat, we shall never die!". But because they did not understand this, the wind blew, the storm beat and the waves arose saying "you are perishing". But Jesus said:

> *50 This is the bread which comes down from heaven, that one may eat of it and not die. [John 6:50]*

When the time of temptation comes, we find ourselves in a storm where we need help because of the weakness we might experience. In the book of Hebrews, we read:

> *18 For in that He Himself has suffered, being tempted, He is able to aid those who are tempted. [Hebrews 2:18]*

And,

> *15 For we do not have a High Priest who cannot sympathize with our weaknesses but was in all [points] tempted as [we are, yet] without sin. [Hebrews 4:15]*

Therefore,

> *16 Let us, therefore, come boldly to the throne of grace, that we may obtain Mercy and find grace to help in time of need. [Hebrews 4:16]*

Because of the misunderstanding of the message of the gospel, some may think that when we come to Jesus, we will never experience any storm in our lives. Therefore, when we find ourselves in the middle of a storm, we easily are disappointed, discouraged and hopeless. As a result, we do not understand why James says in his epistle: *"count it all joy when you fall into various temptation!"*[16]. Let us remember the fact that Jesus was with the disciples in the boat and yet the storm happened. Similarly, He could be in you and you in Him and yet a storm could come. Jesus never promised that there would be no storm. Rather, what He did say is that the end is deliverance and salvation from the storm and not destruction and death. For this reason, you can keep your peace during the storm, looking for Mercy

---

[16] James 1:2

to hold you together and even have rest, just as He did. Both stories of the disciples in the boats in the middle of storms ended with salvation.

In one story[17], Peter started walking on the water, just like Jesus, but suddenly he became frightened by the wind and the waves, and he began to drown. He cried out to Jesus: "Lord save me!". We know from the story that Jesus grabbed him by the hand and they entered the boat together; most probably they both began walking on the water together! From this story we are to learn that even if you are caught in the midst of a storm and are like Peter - drowning in the waves of doubts - Jesus will grab you by the hand once you call on Him and then both of you will walk together on doubts and immediately come back to a mind (the boat) that is peaceful!

Now, concerning temptations, Paul says:

> *13 No temptation has overtaken you except such as is common to man; but God [is] faithful, who will not allow you to be tempted beyond what you are able, but with the temptation will also make the way of escape, that you may be able to bear [it]. [1 Corinthians 10:13]*

James also adds:

> *13 Let no one say when he is tempted, "I am tempted by God"; for God cannot be tempted by evil, nor does He Himself tempt anyone. [James 1:13]*

The temptation is only a doctrine, a voice or even a thought that begins speaking contrary to what God has already said. The purpose of temptation is leading man away from "believing", by causing him to believe another voice rather than God. By doing this, man falls prey to his own works, labours and sufferings.

From the above scriptures we can understand that even though the temptation is common to all men, it is never from God. God is the One

---

[17] Matthew 14:28-31

who makes a way out of it for us. This is what James says in verse 12, that enduring temptation leads to life and not destruction:

> *12 Blessed [is] the man who endures temptation; for when he has been approved, he will receive the crown of life which the Lord has promised to those who love Him. [James 1:12]*

That is why we can count it all joy when we are in temptations:

> *2 My brethren, count it all joy when you fall into various trials [temptation]. [James 1:2]*

But he also continues to say that after you have endured temptation, you will be perfect and lack nothing:

> *3 Knowing that the testing of your faith produces patience. 4 But let patience have [its] perfect work, that you may be perfect and complete, lacking nothing. [James 1:3-4]*

Unlike common understanding, times of temptation are not meant to bring sufferings or death, but rather, perfection – for it is a "Perfect Man" who lacks nothing. Enduring a temptation does not mean having to suffer through tolerating evil. On the contrary, it means to persevere and hold on to God's truth and His Mercy which will deliver us from every temptation.

Times of temptation are where we become partakers of His sufferings so that we may not fall into our own sufferings, being ruled by temptation. It is the time when we can truly stand and believe in what He suffered for and, thus, receive the glory that is available for us because of His suffering.

Peter writes:

> *12 Beloved, do not think it strange concerning the fiery trial [temptation] which is to try you, as though some strange thing happened to you; 13 but rejoice to the extent that you partake of Christ's sufferings, that when His glory is revealed, you may also be glad with exceeding joy. [1 Peter 4:12-13]*

Here we see that enduring temptation to receive the crown of life and appear in His glory is achieved by partaking of His suffering. The word "partaking" means "to come into communion or fellowship with". In other words, partaking of His suffering is to have fellowship with His suffering in the time of temptation in order to be able to enter His rest. This does not mean to suffer in our own sufferings, but rather, to partake of His suffering. I will explain and expand on this further, as we go along.

Now this "partaking" refers to a kind of "fellowship" we have with His suffering. According to Hebrews 2:9, this suffering is the "suffering of death":

> *9 But we see Jesus, who was made a little lower than the angels, for the suffering of death crowned with glory and honour, that He, by the grace of God, might taste death for everyone. [Hebrews 2:9]*

Therefore "partaking" or "fellowship" of His suffering refers to His death, where His body was broken and His blood was shed. Thus, we have fellowship with His body which was broken for us and His blood which was shed for us. The way we fellowship with His body and blood is the eating of His body as the true bread and drinking of His blood as the true drink, which give life. This is explained by Paul in his letter to the church at Corinth:

> *16 The cup of blessing which we bless, is it not the communion [fellowship] of the blood of Christ? The bread which we break, is it not the communion [fellowship] of the body of Christ? [1 Corinthians 10:16]*

The word "communion" also means "fellowship" or "intimacy"[18]. When Paul speaks of having the communion of bread and wine, he is actually referring to having fellowship with His body and blood, thus with His death, or in other words, with His suffering. This is the meaning of "partaking of His suffering".

In eating the bread as His body and drinking the cup of blessing as His blood, we remember what He accomplished for us on the cross:

---

[18] G2842 - Translated 12 time as "fellowship" in the King James Version and only 4 times as "communion".

> *24 And when He had given thanks, He broke [it] and said, "Take, eat; this is My body which is broken for you; do this in remembrance of Me." 25 In the same manner [He] also [took] the cup after supper, saying, "This cup is the new covenant in My blood. This do, as often as you drink [it], in remembrance of Me." [1 Corinthians 11:24-25]*

We remember "Him" and not our sin, nor our weakness, not even the trials and temptations; we remember Him. As often as we eat bread or drink the wine, we should remember what He has done for us. We remember the suffering of death that He went through for us so that He would also bring us to His glory, and not to the suffering:

> *9 But we see Jesus, who was made a little lower than the angels, for the suffering of death crowned with glory and honour, that He, by the grace of God, might taste death for everyone. 10 For it was fitting for Him, for whom [are] all things and by whom [are] all things, in bringing many sons to glory, to make the captain of their salvation perfect through sufferings. [Hebrews 2:9-10]*

These verses clearly show that He went through the suffering of death for everyone; that He would also bring them into His glory. These people were called the "Sons" in "Glory".

Nevertheless, for these sons to enter God's glory, it is only the suffering of Jesus that was necessary and not their own suffering. However, these sons, while growing up into the fullness of Christ and His glory, must continuously partake of His sufferings by remembering His death. This is what Paul calls the "Communion of the Lord". It is practiced in churches ritually, but it is powerless if one's understanding of the practice does not accompany the action. It is the revelation of the death of Jesus that enables us to "partake" of His death and be free from our past, weaknesses, sicknesses, sin and death itself. It is through our understanding of this revelation that we are empowered to endure temptations, rather than succumb to them. By partaking of His suffering, which is His death, we proclaim His death. When death comes, we do not receive it but stand in the truth that He died and we died with Him. Paul says we must continue to do this "until" He comes. This "coming" is the coming of "glory" or, in other words, is when He comes to bring us to His glory.

> *26 For as often as you eat this bread and drink this cup, you proclaim the Lord's death till He comes. [1 Corinthians 11:26]*

While here on earth, Jesus was tempted in all sorts of ways, but He never bowed down or succumbed to temptation. He suffered, not because He had sinned, but because we had sinned by falling into temptation. This is why He now helps those who are being tempted by empowering them to overcome any temptation and not fall into sin and its sufferings. He took the sufferings related to temptations upon Himself so that we would never again experience the suffering but instead, His glory:

> *18 For in that He Himself has suffered, being tempted, He is able to aid those who are tempted. [Hebrews 2:18]*

Now let us go back to the story of Paul in the storm, in Acts 27. We want to see how he and all other souls in the ship were eventually saved because Paul "partook of the sufferings of Christ".

Being in a strong tempest storm, they did all they could do, to help the ship to endure the storm. They undergirded the ship with cables, lightened it and even threw the ship's tackle overboard with their own hand. For many days they did not see the sun, nor did the stars appear. They finally gave up hope and did not even eat anything during those days:

> *33 And as day was about to dawn, Paul implored [them] all to take food, saying, "Today is the fourteenth day <u>you</u> have waited and continued without food, and eaten nothing. 34 Therefore I urge you to take nourishment, for this is for your survival, since not a hair will fall from the head of any of you." [Acts 27:33-34]*

But if we pay close attention to these verses, we realize that none of them had eaten any food for a long time, except for Paul. He told them: *"you have waited and continued without food and eaten nothing"*. This implies that he himself was eating food in the days of the tempest. In order to encourage them to eat, he took bread, broke it and began to eat. It was then that they all ate:

> *35 And when he had said these things, he took bread and gave thanks to God in the presence of them all; and when he had broken [it] he began to eat. 36 Then they were all encouraged, and also took food themselves. [Acts 27:35-36]*

No one had eaten during the tempest storm because of their discouragement and fear of death. But in the midst of the storm, Paul was instead breaking the "bread" and "eating" of it, "remembering" His sufferings. That is why he, unlike the others, did not lose hope and remained encouraged:

> *20 Now when neither sun nor stars appeared for many days, and no small tempest beat on [us], <u>all hope that we would be saved was finally given up</u>. 21 But <u>after long abstinence from food</u>, then Paul stood in the midst of them and said, "Men, you should have listened to me, and not have sailed from Crete and incurred this disaster and loss." [Acts 27:20-21]*

Earlier on in this chapter, we discussed that the reason the disciples were caught in the storm was that they did not understand the multiplying of the bread. This is why Jesus, immediately after rescuing them from the storm, began talking to them about the bread of life: "His body". His body is the body that was broken on the cross for us; it is His body that went through the sufferings of death. From this, we are to know and believe that in the time of temptations - when the storms and tempest waves rise - if we partake of His suffering by eating His body, remembering His death and suffering for us, we will not lose hope for salvation. Rather, we can stay encouraged - which is when a message will come to us from the Lord to confirm our salvation, just as it did to Paul:

> *22 And now I urge you to take heart, for there will be no loss of life among you, but only of the ship. 23 For there stood by me this night an angel of the God to whom I belong and whom I serve, 24 saying, <u>"Do not be afraid, Paul</u>; you must be brought before Caesar; and indeed, God has granted you all those who sail with you." 25*

> *Therefore take heart, men, for I believe God that it will be just as it was told me. [Acts 27:22-25]*

At the end of this story, there was the salvation of every soul who was on the ship. The only loss the disciples experienced was that of the ship itself.

Even though they had girded the ship with the cable (which, as we have learned, symbolizes the Mercy of God), along the way they lost hope and became discouraged because they did not "continue" to eat of His bread and remember how He had suffered for them. While this eventually resulted in the loss of the ship itself, it did not result in the loss of any souls. Because of one person, Paul, who continued in partaking of Christ's suffering, all of the two hundred and six souls on the ship were saved. In the midst of those terrifying days, when there seemed to be no hope for them, there was one on the boat who was full of hope. He stayed encouraged and endured temptation by breaking the bread of life. He partook of His suffering by remembering His death. He ate from His body that was broken for them and thus stood in faith and continued to believe that because Jesus had tasted the suffering of death for everyone, this storm was not going to end with death, but rather, with salvation.

All of their souls were saved because Paul continued in the partaking of Christ's suffering; he did not forget His Mercy but, instead, continued in His fellowship. Paul not only endured the temptation for himself, but he also brought salvation for others just as the angel told him: *"and indeed, God has granted you all those who sail with you"*.

The will of God for us is - to understand the bread and the sacrifice of His body, so that we can endure every temptation, stay encouraged, keep holding on to His Mercy and believe for salvation; not only for ourselves but also for those who are yet to come to know His suffering of death. That is why we read in the book of Ephesians that growing in the truth and knowledge of Christ is essential for us.

We all need to grow up to be a "Perfect Man" who lacks nothing. As long as we remain immature "children", we will have temptations which come to us from different winds of doctrines. Thankfully God, in His grace and Mercy, has appointed and given us "gifts" to bring us to this perfection:

> *11 And He Himself gave some [to be] apostles, some prophets, some evangelists, and some pastors and teachers, 12 for the equipping of the saints for the work of ministry, for the edifying of the body of Christ, 13 till we all come to the unity of the faith and of the knowledge of the Son of God, to a perfect man, to the measure of the stature of the fullness of Christ; 14 that we should no longer be children, tossed to and fro and carried about with every wind of doctrine, by the trickery of men, in the cunning craftiness of deceitful plotting. [Ephesians 4:11-14]*

Thus, every gift has been given to us to make us mature and perfect in all things as the "Perfect Man", just as Christ Himself. The gifts that have been given to us from the Lord are from Him to equip and edify us, until we all come to the place of the unity of faith and the unity of the knowledge of the Son of God, to the measure of the stature of the fullness of Christ. This is the place that is "*the other side*"; the place that He has told us to go to and the place we head toward. Until then, our ship might experience storms along the way but He who is faithful has promised and will come to our aid by bringing His Mercy and taking us to "*the other side*": our Salvation.

This chapter has been the hardest chapter for me to write because even though the solution to escape the corruption of humanity seems to be easy, simple and attainable, I am also aware of the pains, struggles, weaknesses and difficulties that we all go through in our lives. I understand that our times of weakness feel real to us. Such times can be extremely difficult for us and many of us experience suffering because of it. But if we do not embrace an alternate solution, we are left to keep repeating this cycle, with no hope of change and overcoming.

The simplicity of the gospel, which is the power of God, must be at the forefront of our thoughts and in our lives; it is a way of thinking and living that brings us life, not death. When we know this, in the midst of any storm we are able to hold on to the Mercy of God and know that His Mercy will hold our ship together so that we can endure the storm. Along the way, we can remain encouraged, eat of His "bread", believe in His salvation, and be at rest while the storm is passing away.

Mercy, The Comfort of the Flood

We read in Psalm 119 verse 76:

> *76 Let, I pray, your Merciful kindness be for my comfort, According to Your word to Your servant. [Psalm 119:76]*

The word "Merciful kindness" in the original Hebrew language is the word "Mercy". Basically, the Psalmist says: *"let, I pray, Your Mercy be for my comfort..."* thereby acknowledging that Mercy brings "comfort" to us.

This comfort is according to His word which means His word is spoken and sent out to bring comfort to mankind by showing them Mercy.

Now let us look at the word "comfort", in Hebrew, to have a deeper understanding of this verse. The Hebrew word is "nacham" (H5162), which is a verb. It is translated 57 times as "comfort" and 41 times as "repent" in the King James translation. A better definition based on its usage in the Bible is:

To experience a comfort or release through a repentance, a change or a reversing.

The first time this word, comfort, is used in the Bible is Genesis 5, where Noah was born and named by his parents:

> *29 And he called his name Noah, saying, "This [one] will comfort us concerning our work and the toil of our hands, because of the ground which the LORD has cursed." [Genesis 5:29]*

Noah's parents gave him a name that meant "comfort". By doing so, they prophesied over him saying: *"this one will bring a comfort from our works and from the toils of our hands"*. The prophecy through Noah's name was not limited to only a specific group of people. Rather, it included comfort for all those in the world who had fallen into works and toil due to the "cursed ground".

We need to take note that Lamech, Noah's father who had named Noah, said it was the Lord who had "cursed the ground". However, if we read Genesis 3, where the "ground was cursed", we come to understand that the ground was cursed for Adam's sake! It was not the Lord who had cursed the ground; it was Adam - Lamech's own forefather! Here we see that Lamech was doing what his forefather had done: "Blaming God!".

> *17 Then to Adam He said, "Because you have heeded the voice of your wife and have eaten from the tree of which I commanded you, saying, 'You shall not eat of it'; Cursed [is] the ground for your sake; In toil you shall eat [of] it all the days of your life." [Genesis 3:17]*

The Lord continues to reveal the consequences of what Adam had done before the consequences manifested:

> *18 Both thorns and thistles it shall bring forth for you, and you shall eat the herb of the field. 19 In the sweat of your face you shall eat bread till you return to the ground, for out of it you were taken; For dust you [are], And to dust, you shall return." [Genesis 3:18-19]*

All who were born from Adam's lineage found themselves in the same curse that Adam had brought into the world. The toil, hard work and sweat that had come upon mankind was because of the "cursed ground" which happened in the time of Adam. Therefore, the "comfort" would have to come through a "changing" or a "reversing" of the land which was cursed. In other words, if the ground could be blessed, man would be blessed and released from his toiling.

Since the "cursing of the ground" and the "toiling of man" came through one man, the redemption from the curse must come through another man. This is why Noah (the 10th man from Adam and the one whose name had a prophesy to fulfill), was the man to bring comfort to all mankind.

Genesis 6 tells us that the Lord saw that the earth was filled with corruption, violence and evil. He decided to destroy the earth, but Noah found grace in the sight of God. Therefore, the Lord told Noah to build an ark so that he and all those of his household could go in the ark and be saved through the Flood. We know the rest of the story; the Flood came and through a series of events finally, the waters began to dry up and Noah's ark rested on top of a mountain that is called "Ararat". The Name "Ararat" means "Curse Reversed"!

Noah's ark rested on a mountain that is called "Cursed Reversed". Therefore, this comfort comes to all mankind through the "reversing of the curse" in the ground. The curse is reversed through the waters. These waters cleansed the earth from unrighteousness, evil and everything that was cursed because of Adam.

The Flood of Noah was the fulfillment of the prophecy of his name: "He shall bring comfort", pointing at "another Flood" that was to come and cleanse the earth from all unrighteousness. The Flood of Noah foreshadowed Christ and what was going to come through Him, as revealed by Peter the apostle:

> *18 For Christ also suffered once for sins, the just for the unjust, that He might bring us to God, being put to death in the flesh but made alive by the Spirit, 19 by whom also He went and preached to the spirits in prison, 20 who formerly were disobedient, when once the Divine longsuffering waited in the days of Noah, while [the] ark was being prepared, in which a few, that is, eight souls, were saved through water. 21 There is also an antitype which now saves us-baptism (not the removal of the filth of the flesh, but the answer of a good conscience toward God), through the resurrection of Jesus*

Christ, 22 who has gone into heaven and is at the right hand of God, angels and authorities and powers having been made subject to Him. [1 Peter 3:18-22]

We mentioned earlier that every single story of the old points at the truth which is "in Jesus Christ". If Noah and his kind of Flood could truly bring comfort to mankind, then there was no need for another day in future that would make "comfort and rest" available:

11 Let us, therefore, be diligent to enter that rest, lest anyone fall according to the same example of disobedience. [Hebrews 4:11]

We can, therefore, understand that the Flood of Noah was symbolic of a future cleansing. The message of the Flood is not destruction. Rather, the Flood provided "Cleansing" and "Salvation" from every curse and, through doing so, brought with it rest and comfort. From this we are also to understand that there is to be another Flood - this time not of Noah, but of Christ - coming to the whole earth, to bring cleansing from all unrighteousness and reversing the curse in the land, thereby bringing comfort.

Peter tells us that this "Flood" was a foreshadowing of our "baptism" in Jesus Christ, for our "Salvation of Soul"! This is beautifully explained in 1 Peter 3:18-22. This baptism is not an external washing and is not for cleansing dirt off of the flesh. To be more precise, it is an "internal washing" and a necessary "cleansing" in our conscience:

21 There is also an antitype which now saves us-baptism (not the removal of the filth of the flesh, but the answer of a good conscience toward God), through the resurrection of Jesus Christ. [1 Peter 3:21]

Before proceeding any further, let us next take a look at the word "answer" in the original language. The Greek word means: "earnestly seeking, craving or having an intense desire". Verse 21 reveals that our baptism in Christ "saves" us by cleansing our conscience from all unrighteousness and causing us to earnestly seek and have a desire for a "Good Conscience" toward God. Because this good conscience is all that is required to save our soul, just as the ark saved eight souls, this baptism in Christ brings the "Salvation of our Soul" through our good conscience.

The Flood of Noah cleansed the earth from all unrighteousness. Baptism in Christ cleanses "our earth" from all unrighteousness, beginning with "our conscience". Because our conscience is where all evil, unrighteousness and death originate, there is therefore also a progression toward our salvation and a completion of our salvation. Salvation comes to us at the end of faith and not at the beginning of our faith in Christ. Peter refers to this completion as the end of faith for the "Salvation of Souls":

9 Receiving the end of your faith- the salvation of [your] souls. [1 Peter 1:9]

On one hand, Peter says here that the cleansing of our conscience through baptism brings us our salvation. But on the other hand, he is also telling us that such salvation is received at the end of faith. This means that baptism in Christ causes one to have faith and walk in faith because of the good conscience created through the "Waters of Flood". In other words, once our faith is perfected through baptism, our salvation is received. We can, therefore, see that a clean conscience that comes through the baptism causes us to live by faith and at the end of our faith is the salvation of our soul.

When scripture says "the end of faith", there must also then be a "beginning of faith" as well. The beginning of faith refers to when we first met Jesus and received the forgiveness of our sins. Until then we were kept under the law, living not by faith but by the works of our own hand because the law is not of faith:

12 Yet the law is not of faith, but "the man who does them shall live by them." [Galatians 3:12]

The law was only a tutor to keep us until we come to Christ and meet faith. Christ introduced the faith:

23 But <u>before faith came</u>, we were <u>kept under guard by the law</u>, <u>kept for the faith</u> which would afterward be revealed. 24 Therefore the *law was our tutor [to bring us] to Christ, that we might be justified by faith. 25 But after faith has come, we are no longer under a tutor. [Galatians 3:23-25]*

When we come to Jesus, we realize that our works were never able to save us; only the faith in Jesus Christ can save us. It is through this faith that we are then called "Sons of God":

26 For you are all sons of God through faith in Christ Jesus. 27 For as many of you as were baptized into Christ have put on Christ. [Galatians 3:26-27]

Since Christ is the end of the law[19], the beginning of our faith was meeting Jesus on the cross for the first time. It was when we realized, by His death, that He had put an end to the works of the law and redeemed us from the curse of the law that faith began:

13 Christ has redeemed us from the curse of the law, having become a curse for us (for it is written, "Cursed [is] everyone who hangs on a tree"), 14 that the blessing of Abraham might come upon the Gentiles in Christ Jesus, that we might receive the promise of the Spirit through faith. [Galatians 3:13-14]

We are to see and understand that the death of Jesus is the end of the law and the beginning of faith. Through "His death", at the beginning of our faith, we were only reconciled to God.

Since we are justified through His blood (shed on the cross at His death) we are called "righteous" or "just". According to scripture, the "just" shall live by faith[20].

At the end of our faith, we will receive the salvation of our soul which, in other words, is to "be saved by His life". It is by His blood that we are kept righteous so that we can keep walking in faith with Him until we arrive at the end of our faith, which is the salvation of our soul:

---

[19] Romans 10:4 "For Christ [is] the end of the law for righteousness for everyone who believes."
[20] Romans 1:17

> *9 Much more then, having now been justified by His blood, we shall be saved from wrath through Him. 10 For if when we were enemies we were **reconciled** to God through the **death** of His Son, much more, having been reconciled, we shall be **saved** by **His life**. [Romans 5:9-10]*

Our walk of faith is from "His Death" to "His Life": His death brings us reconciliation to God; His life brings us salvation.

Now let us turn to the "baptism in Christ" (the answer of a good conscience), where Paul clarifies that it is "baptism into His death":

> *3 Or do you not know that as many of us as were baptized into Christ Jesus were baptized into His death? [Romans 6:3]*

Our baptism into His death enables us to partake of His life also:

> *4 Therefore we were buried with Him through baptism into death, that just as Christ was raised from the dead by the glory of the Father, even so, we also should walk in newness of life. 5 For if we have been united together in the likeness of His death, certainly we also shall be [in the likeness] of [His] resurrection. [Romans 6:4-5]*

According to Paul, there is only one thing that helps us to walk in the "newness of life" and that is "to be baptized into His death". If there is no death "with Him", there will be no resurrection "with Him". The resurrection of Jesus from the dead is the newness of life that we can live in. But in order to walk in the newness of life, we must be raised anew, after the death and burial of our former selves "with Christ":

> *6 Knowing this, that our old man was crucified with [Him], that the body of sin might be done away with, that we should no longer be slaves of sin. 7 For he who has died has been freed from sin. [Romans 6:6-7]*

Baptism into "His death" brings us into newness and allows us to live in "His Resurrection Life". We also read in 1 Peter that baptism brings us salvation. The kind of "salvation" that both Peter and Paul repeatedly speak of is "Resurrection Life" or, in other words, our partaking of "His Resurrected Life":

> *5 For if we have been united together in the likeness of His death, certainly we also shall be [in the likeness] of [His] resurrection. [Romans 6:5]*

We need also to remember that this salvation comes to us as the result of a cleansed-conscience, through partaking of His death. Through His blood, His death provides the means by which our conscience is cleansed from every unrighteousness and uncleanness.

When Jesus was asked by His disciples concerning His coming (Matthew 24), He told them that no one would know the hour and that it would be like the "Flood in the days of Noah". We have also, by now, come to understand that this Flood is baptism into His death, purposed to bring salvation to mankind.

Salvation is a personal encounter that happens to each individual. That is why the time and hour is not known by anyone. The coming of Jesus for a second time is, therefore, for the purpose of bringing salvation to those who have been continuously partaking of His death, having their conscience cleansed and walking in faith to the end where they receive that promised salvation.

As the book of Hebrews also says:

> *28 So, Christ was offered once to bear the sins of many, to those who eagerly wait for Him, He will appear the second time, apart from sin for salvation. [Hebrews 9:28]*

This verse clearly shows us that salvation comes because He offered Himself to bring cleansing of sin by way of baptism into His death. His second coming, however, will be for the purpose of salvation to save those who are waiting for him and not for the purpose of cleansing or taking sin away.

For clarity purposes, salvation is not what is now commonly referred to as "new birth". Rather, our "new birth" is a "new beginning" or "starting point" of our salvation and is, therefore, "the reconciliation to God". This is because our "new birth" is received by us through the cleansing of our sin; it is at the completion of the work of faith within us that our salvation truly and fully takes place.

Verse 28 clearly tells us that this salvation will be received by *"those who eagerly wait for Him"* – meaning those who have learnt to partake of His death and have been living by baptism into His death, letting His death wash and cleanse their conscience from all unrighteousness. It is to them that He will appear a second time to bring salvation. It is important to note that scripture does not say "for the last time"; rather, it says "for a second time". The emphasis on the "second time" is to distinguish it from the first time. The first appearance was for taking away sin by offering Himself as the sacrificial Lamb. When He appears again, He will not come as a Lamb to take away sin. Rather, He will appear a second time as a Lion, to bring salvation as a result of the removal of sin.

The second time will not be the only or the last time; there will be many "second times". Jesus comes in our lives to bring salvation by helping us to continue walking in faith, enduring and overcoming temptations and thus receiving the crown of life which is the salvation of our souls.

We read in the book of Hebrews that the sacrifices that were offered up under the old system of the law were only symbolic, pointing at the truth which would come in Christ Jesus. Those sacrifices could never reach out to the most inner part of a man - man's conscience, to cleanse it. Thus, such sacrifices were powerless in making anyone perfect:

> *9 It [was] symbolic for the present time in which both gifts and sacrifices are offered which cannot make him who performed the service perfect in regard to the conscience. [Hebrews 9:9]*

And,

> *1 For the law, having a shadow of the good things to come, [and] not the very image of the things, can never with these same sacrifices, which they offer continually year by year, make those who approach perfect. 2 For then would they not have ceased to be offered? For the worshipers, once purified, would have had no more consciousness of sins. [Hebrews 10:1-2]*

Also,

> *14 How much more shall the blood of Christ, who through the eternal Spirit offered Himself without spot to God, cleanse your conscience from dead works to serve the living God? [Hebrews 9:14]*

Chapters 9 and 10 of the book of Hebrews indicate that the issue of sin is not on the outside of ourselves, but rather, on the inside of our own conscience. The reason animal sacrifices - or any other sacrifices - cannot cleanse or remove sin is because they do not have access to the conscience, which is where sin resides and operates.

We also read that not only did those sacrifices not remove sin, they also served as a reminder of sin, thereby giving sin even more power to work in the lives of these people.

The solution to take away sin and fruits of it in the life of people is not to cleanse the outside, which is the actions of people, but rather, to cleanse the inside, which is the conscience. What is often called "sin" is the external action of people. These actions are only the visible manifestation of something that comes from within their own conscience and are the "fruit" of sin. If we keep removing the fruits, without uprooting the tree, it will continue to produce more of the same kind fruits. Jesus came to uproot the tree so that the full issue of sin could be resolved. That is why we read in the beginning of Hebrews 10 that bringing sacrifices does not cause the conscience, where the tree of sin abides, to be cleansed; such cleansing is done through the "blood" of Jesus Christ.

Sin is an issue in the conscience that must be cleansed. As long as the conscience is aware of sin, or is polluted by sin, one's actions will be controlled by it; this is how sin "rules and reigns" in one's body. The reigning of sin is in the conscience. Jesus came to resolve this abnormal situation; not focusing to fix the outside, but rather the inside: the conscience. Doing this affects the outside and cleanses it accordingly, just as He told the Pharisees when He said, "you clean the outside of the cup, but inside is full of dirt[21]". Here He was referring to those who were keeping the rituals according to the law and showing themselves pure on the outside. This is what religion does! It deals with the outside appearance of man which never changes or transforms a man. In fact, because there is defilement on the inside, man acts the way he does.

Down through the ages and generations, religion has focused on making the action of people good - but Jesus came to deal with the root and not the fruit. He came to heal the sick; not to offer temporary remedies. Jesus came to awaken mankind again by raising them up from the dust of the ground and taking away what was causing them to labour and later die: Sin!

As Romans chapter 8 says:

> *1 [There is] therefore now no condemnation to those who are in Christ Jesus, who do not walk according to the flesh, but according to the Spirit. 2 For the law of the Spirit of life in Christ Jesus has made me free from the law of sin and death. [Romans 8:1-2]*

He brought a "New" law which supercedes the old law. It is called: "the law of the Spirit of Life". However, this new law must replace the old law: "the law of Sin and Death". Sin snuck into the conscience of man, bearing fruit to death, in his body. But now the new law has arrived! Since the new law replaces the old law which started in the conscience, followed by manifestation in the body, the new law must first replace the old law in the conscience of man. Once this is done, man will have life in his body as well.

Just as sin reigns through conscience, so too must life reign through the conscience! In order for life to take the place of sin, the sin must die and become buried so that we are set free from its dominance and, instead, come under the new supremacy of life. This is the truth about our co-crucifixion with Christ on the cross. We died with Him! It is essential that we have continuous awareness of this; that we see it as

[21] Matthew 23:25

"our truth" and that we live under this truth. We must consider this as the only truth about ourselves, otherwise, we are deceiving ourselves.

Seeing ourselves in the light of this truth in every moment, cleanses the conscience from sin and dead works. He, at His death, crucified the old man, the man of sin which was ruling over us, and by shedding His blood, He cleansed our conscience from sin which was producing dead works.

Earlier we mentioned that when we were baptized into Christ Jesus, we were actually baptized into His death. This means that our burial with Jesus was when we were baptized into His death. In other words, when Jesus was buried, we too were buried with Him - but the person who was buried was the one who was also crucified. The one who was crucified was the old man and this old man was the one who was under the power of sin, whose body was a slave to sin.

Sin had power over our conscience and was manifesting itself in the seen realm, which is our body. But through baptism into His death, we put an end to the old man with its old way of thinking, all of its desires, habits of flesh and the old conscience which was governed by sin. This is not the end of the story, but rather, the beginning of the gospel of Jesus Christ! Just as His death happened for us, so also did His resurrection for us.

This is what apostle Paul writes to Timothy, reminding him of his gospel:

> *8 Remember that Jesus Christ, of the seed of David, was raised from the dead according to my gospel. [2 Timothy 2:8]*

The good news for mankind is the resurrection of Jesus Christ. His resurrection is the only way of bringing "newness of life" for us; His resurrection is the "comfort" and the "rest" that was to come to all men because the enemy of mankind, death, was put under His feet at the resurrection.

We read in Romans 6 that death was the wages of sin:

23 For the wages of sin [is] death, but the gift of God [is] eternal life in Christ Jesus our Lord. [Romans 6:23]

We can also read chapter 5 where it tells us how this sin and death entered the world and spread to all:

12 Therefore, just as through one man sin entered the world, and death through sin, and thus death spread to all men because all sinned. [Romans 5:12]

Sin entered the conscience of people, began reigning over them and then asked for its wages of reigning: "death in people's body". Therefore, "death" in the body is the "fruit" of the "tree of sin" that resides in the conscience of people. The fullness of death in a body is when a person dies and their body is buried. But prior to that, the body of that person experiences death in different forms such as pain, weakness, sickness and disease. From this, we see that anything in the body (in the seen realm) that does not produce life is actually death. Corruption, decay and mortality are under the category of death and they are manifested in the body, in the seen realm, but they start by reigning in the conscience.

So, we can easily see that "sin reigns in the conscience" and through sin "death reigns in the body".

The work of sin in the conscience is specifically intended to convince mankind that he is deserving of punishment and death. We can see that clearly in the story of Cain and Abel in Genesis 4:

3 And in the process of time, it came to pass that Cain brought an offering of the fruit of the ground to the LORD. 4 Abel also brought of the firstborn of his flock and of their fat. And the LORD respected Abel and his offering, 5 but He did not respect Cain and his offering. And Cain was very angry, and his countenance fell.

6 So the LORD said to Cain, "Why are you angry? And why has your countenance fallen? 7 If you do well, will you not be accepted? And if you do not do well, sin lies at the door. And its desire [is] for you, but you should rule over it."

> *8 Now Cain talked with Abel his brother; and it came to pass, when they were in the field, that Cain rose up against Abel his brother and killed him.*
>
> *9 Then the LORD said to Cain, "Where [is] Abel your brother?" He said, "I do not know. [Am] I my brother's keeper?"*
>
> *10 And He said, "What have you done? The voice of your brother's blood cries out to Me from the ground. 11 So now you [are] cursed from the earth, which has opened its mouth to receive your brother's blood from your hand. 12 When you till the ground, it shall no longer yield its strength to you. A fugitive and a vagabond you shall be on the earth." [Genesis 4:3-12]*

This is an amazing story because it answers many questions and reveals the truth; yet by the same token, it is a heartbreaking and sad story. It shows us what has been happening to mankind since sin crept in.

Cain first brought a sacrifice to the Lord which was from the fruit of the ground. It was not accepted by the Lord because he took the sacrifice from the ground that was cursed after his father, Adam, who had eaten from the tree of the Knowledge of Good and Evil. He had offered fruit from the cursed ground! Cain had toiled and worked for it and had shed his sweat on that cursed ground; in effect, he had brought the works of his own hand. This kind of offering was not and is not acceptable by the Lord. Had it been, man would have been left to forever toil, labour and curse. The sacrifice that God accepts must be according to the work of God's own hand and not the toiling of man. That is why Abel's sacrifice was accepted. Abel had brought the firstborn of his flock; he had not toiled for it to grow. He was only a shepherd protecting and feeding the sheep. His offering was referring to the true sacrificial Lamb which was to come and take away the sin of the world: "Jesus".

By contrast, because Cain's offering was not accepted, his countenance fell and he became angry. Sin drew near at the door of his conscience, knocking and desiring to enter in. The Lord came and told him that he must "reign over sin", probably by not opening his conscience to sin. But Cain, later on, killed his brother. Sin entered his conscience and asked for its wages: "Death".

After Cain killed his brother, the Lord came to him again and told him what was going to happen as a result:

> *11 So now you [are] cursed from the earth, which has opened its mouth to receive your brother's blood from your hand. 12 When you till the ground, it shall no longer yield its strength to you. A fugitive and a vagabond you shall be on the earth. [Genesis 4:11-12]*

But Cain said:

> *13 And Cain said to the LORD, "My punishment [is] greater than I can bear! 14 Surely You have driven me out this day from the face of the ground; I shall be hidden from Your face; I shall be a fugitive and a vagabond on the earth, and it will happen [that] anyone who finds me will kill me." [Genesis 4:13]*

Take note that the Lord did not tell him that he was deserving of the punishment of death. Rather, it was Cain who judged himself worthy of punishment and death. This is what sin does! It first convinced Cain that his brother was worthy of death and then convinced him that he himself was also worthy of death.

But the Lord put a mark on Cain's forehead to avoid him being killed by anyone:

> *15 And the LORD said to him, "Therefore, whoever kills Cain, vengeance shall be taken on him sevenfold." And the LORD set a mark on Cain, lest anyone finding him should kill him. 16 Then Cain went out from the presence of the LORD and dwelt in the land of Nod on the east of Eden. [Genesis 4:15-16]*

The mark on Cain's forehead protected him from being killed by another. I believe that the mark was put on his conscience so that not only could he be protected from his own thoughts against himself, but also from the judgment of others against the mistake he had made. That is why even though the conscience of every man who has come through Adam is ruled by sin (being convinced of punishment of death), there is also another voice (the mark on their forehead) telling them that they are worthy of life.

That is why all people, starting from the first man, have a knowing within themselves that killing, murdering and destruction is not right. They all seek life, love and peace. However, since sin entered their conscience and began reigning in their body, mankind has been powerless in ruling over sin, and over the course of time death has been a sure end.

God told Cain that because he had shed the blood of his brother on the ground, he was cursed. We need to see that first the ground was cursed (Genesis 3) after Adam ate from the tree of the Knowledge of Good and Evil:

> *17 Then to Adam He said, "Because you have heeded the voice of your wife and have eaten from the tree of which I commanded you, saying, 'You shall not eat of it'; Cursed [is] the ground for your sake; In toil you shall eat [of] it All the days of your life. 18 Both thorns and thistles it shall bring forth for you, and you shall eat the herb of the field. 19 In the sweat of your face you shall eat bread till you return to the ground, for out of it you were taken; For dust you [are], And to dust, you shall return." [Genesis 3:17-19]*

And next we see that the Lord then told Cain that because of what he had done, he was also cursed:

> *11 So now you [are] cursed from the earth, which has opened its mouth to receive your brother's blood from your hand. 12 When you till the ground, it shall no longer yield its strength to you. A fugitive and a vagabond you shall be on the earth. [Genesis 4:11-12]*

Now we want to find out which ground (or earth) the Lord was referring to. Even though it is the ground we know of, it also represents a deeper truth concerning man and his relation to it, in a symbolic way. Let us take a look at this next.

We read in Genesis that God made Adam from the ground:

7 And the LORD God formed man [of] the dust of the ground and breathed into his nostrils the breath of life, and man became a living being. [Genesis 2:7]

We also find in 1 Corinthians 15 that Adam was "of the earth" and made of "dust":

47 The first man [was] of the earth, [made] of dust; the second Man [is] the Lord from heaven. 48 As [was] the [man] of dust, so also [are] those [who are made] of dust; and as [is] the heavenly [Man], so also [are] those [who are] heavenly. [1 Corinthians 15:47-48]

Therefore, if Adam was from the dust of the ground, Adam was dust. If Adam was from the earth, Adam was earth. If we continue reading further it says that Adam was "flesh and blood" and this "flesh and blood" cannot inherit the kingdom of God:

50 Now, this I say, brethren, that flesh and blood cannot inherit the kingdom of God; nor does corruption inherit incorruption. [1 Corinthians 15:50]

From this, we see that Adam, being from "dust" or "earth", refers not only to his whole nature but also specifically to his "body", which is "flesh and blood". Therefore, the "body" of Adam is also "the earth" or "the ground"!

So now, when the ground was cursed in Genesis 3, it was not only referring to the ground as we know it but primarily to "Adam's body" as well. Let us bear in mind that sin entered the conscience of man and the fruit of sin, being death, came to his body. Therefore, the curse entered the body of mankind causing them to be ruled by death.

As we have discussed previously, because this whole corruption came through one man - Adam- and ultimately spread to all mankind and all died, its reversal and removal must also come through One Man, spreading to all man, so that all can live. Since there was no man who could do this, because all men were under the reign of sin, He Himself became "flesh and blood" so that He could destroy the works of sin in the body of mankind, reversing the curse from the ground and bringing comfort. This is Jesus!

In order to redeem those who are born from Adam, Jesus had to come in the likeness of "Adam's body", which is "flesh and blood", to shed His own blood on the same ground which was cursed by man and thereby redeem the ground from the curse. He was crucified and shed His blood on the same ground which had been cursed from the time of the first man – Adam. But this time, however, the ground received blood that was shed willingly and not unjustly. He shed His blood on the same ground and then cried out loud, releasing forgiveness and Mercy, so that the curse can be removed from the body of mankind:

> *33 And when they had come to the place called Calvary, there they crucified Him, and the criminals, one on the right hand and the other on the left. 34 Then Jesus said, "Father, forgive them, for they do not know what they do." And they divided His garments and cast lots. [Luke 23:33-34]*

When He was resurrected, coming out of death, the curse in the land (the body) was reversed. Because He was raised from the dead, death has no power over Him and He shall never go to corruption.

Earlier in the chapter, we spoke about the "Flood of Noah" which was a symbol - a foreshadowing - of the "baptism in His death". The ark had landed on a mountain that had come out of the Flood; the mountain was named "Ararat", which means: "Curse Reversed". We also learned earlier that if the "Flood of Noah" is symbolic of "His death", then the "Mountain coming out" of the Flood is symbolic of "His Resurrection out of death" in the body. In other words, at the resurrection of Jesus, the curse in the body of man (the ground) is now reversed! What had started in one Man, Jesus, must also be spread to all men, similar to what happened through Adam. This is the fulfilment of the "comfort" and "rest" for mankind, as it was prophesied through Noah:

> *29 And he called his name Noah, saying, "This [one] <u>will comfort us</u> concerning our work and the toil of our hands, because of the <u>ground</u> which the LORD has <u>cursed</u>." [Genesis 5:29]*

When Jesus was resurrected, He was raised to a New Man- out of the old body (old earth) into a new body (new earth). This New Man is where the old heaven and earth are no more, but the new Heaven and Earth have come to where righteousness dwells (2 Peter 3:13) because His death washed away all unrighteousness!

Through the resurrection of Jesus, the New Man is where "comfort" has entered and man is released from the toiling of his own hand because the curse was now reversed. His resurrection from the dead can be compared to the ascending of the mountain through the waters of the Flood. His body, which is now a "new body" or the "body of glory" filled with Spirit, came out of the Flood of His own blood which He shed so that mountains (the curse-reversed bodies) could now be resurrected through His Flood, being His death.

If His death is for us or, in other words, He died as us, then His resurrection is the good news (the gospel) for us and we can confidently now say that He is resurrected "as us". This is why Paul continues to re-iterate in Romans 6 that if we were united with Him in His death and burial, certainly we must be united with Him in His resurrection and life as well. In other words, just as we died to sin with Him, we now must live with and for Him.

We cannot stop at His death and not believe in the resurrection. We cannot believe that His death was for us and His resurrection was not! Jesus died to sin, but He was raised by the power of God and, therefore, this is our story as well:

> *8 Now if we died with Christ, we believe that we shall also live with Him, 9 knowing that Christ, having been raised from the dead, dies no more. Death no longer has dominion over Him. 10 For [the death] that He died, He died to sin once for all; but [the life] that He lives, He lives to God. [Romans 6:8-10]*

If His physical body that died on that cross was our body that died, His resurrected body shall be our body also; being resurrected out of the old into the new body, and out of the old man to the new man.

20 For our citizenship is in heaven, from which we also eagerly wait for the Savior, the Lord Jesus Christ, 21 who will transform our lowly body that it may be conformed to His glorious body, according to the working by which He is able even to subdue all things to Himself. [Philippians 3:20-21]

Christ died to sin but He is now raised from the dead and dies no more because death no longer has dominion over Him. His death was death to sin once for all, but His life is a life that lives to God. Therefore, the baptism into His death is our death to sin. In other words, through baptism in His death we put an end to sin, therefore, sin has died in its own trap: Death!

Our death in baptism is basically the death of sin. But just as Christ is raised from the dead we must also partake of the same, but now in a new body:

8 Now if we died with Christ, we believe that we shall also live with Him, 9 knowing that Christ, having been raised from the dead, dies no more. Death no longer has dominion over Him. 10 For [the death] that He died, He died to sin once for all; but [the life] that He lives, He lives to God. 11 Likewise you also, reckon yourselves to be dead indeed to sin, but alive to God in Christ Jesus our Lord. [Romans 6:8-11]

Paul says, in a like manner, that we must also "reckon" ourselves to be dead to sin, and "reckon" ourselves to be alive to God. Our death has happened in the past and now it is time to live "with Him" in His resurrection life; the kind of life over which death has no power!

Let us now look at the original meaning of the word "reckon" to understand Paul's words in the above verses in a more powerful way. Even though this word is not commonly used in day to day conversations, it is essential to understand what it meant (and means) in the original language. While translators might have used the closest word to explain its meaning, looking at the original meaning of this word can give us a clearer understanding that will help us more accurately interpret this part of the scripture.

The Greek word for "reckon" is "*logizomai*"; it is a verb which means: "to consider, to meditate on, to take into account, or even to judge". This word refers more to a fact than a thought, assumption, supposition or opinion.[22] One can have an opinion, idea or assumption about something and consider and think about it, but this word is not referring to that. The word's intent is to give consideration to a "fact" that is a "truth"; by not doing so, one is otherwise deceiving oneself.

Paul tells us that our death in Christ (dying to the old man), and our burial with Him is a fact and a truth that we must deem (reckon) to be a true fact; for us to have any other thoughts or considerations that are contrary to this "truth" places us in a position of deceiving ourselves! We are to walk in this newness of life and not be bound to the old man whom we've crucified and buried with Jesus. We have been raised with Jesus from the dead and because death has no power over Him, neither does it have power over us. Just as He lives to God, we live to God also! Therefore, we are to reckon ourselves as dead to sin and alive to God; by doing otherwise, we deceive and rob ourselves from the truth about who we are in Christ Jesus!

Paul goes on to say:

12 Therefore do not let sin reign in your mortal body, that you should obey it in its lusts. [Romans 6:12]

We have clearly seen that "not reckoning" ourselves dead to sin causes sin to reign in our bodies. On the other hand, however, the fact is that the body of sin was crucified on that cross with Jesus and was buried. Sin, therefore, cannot come alive again to take authority over our bodies. Knowing this, we are to stand tall and not allow sin to be a thief that steals from us, deceptively and deceitfully, that which does not belong to it.

13 And do not present your members [as] instruments of unrighteousness to sin but present yourselves to God as being alive from the dead, and your members [as] instruments of righteousness

[22] The definition of this word is taken from Strong's Concordance G3049 from the Blue Letter Bible (www.blueletterbible.org)

to God. 14 For sin shall not have dominion over you, for you are not under law but under grace. [Romans 6:13-14]

Presenting every part of ourselves as instruments of righteousness happens when we do not let sin reign over our body by "reckoning" ourselves dead to sin, and alive to God. By doing this, we allow God to reign over our entire body and all of the parts of our entire being formulate instruments of righteousness.

Sin has dominion over the body as long as man is under the law. However, since we have been freed from the law, sin will no longer have dominion over us. So, we can see here that sin reigns through the power of the law. This tells us that if there is a working of sin, manifested through any kind of corruption, seen in the body, there must be a law in place that empowers sin in continuing to reign. This law must have been placed by us and not God since He took the law away by baptizing us into the death of Christ. If then Paul says not to let sin reign in our body, he is also referring to the law, meaning we are not to put ourselves under any law made by ourselves. But by remembering that through the grace of God we tasted death with Jesus Christ on that cross, it is by the same grace that we must live and reign in life through His life.

Here is the truth and here is the fact that we must "reckon" to ourselves, just as it is true about Jesus:

"Death, Burial and Resurrection"

This "reckoning" is internal, related to our thinking, consideration and judgment. We can further say that it is related to our conscience. This way of thinking causes the baptism in His death to start working in us and, initiating the cleansing of our conscience from sin, which in turn cleanses the flesh from death (the fruit of sin). As we have learnt, this happens because of His blood that was shed at His death, which has the power to remove sin from our conscience. Therefore, we can say that by "reckoning" ourselves dead to the old man, the sin, we cleanse our conscience from the old so that we can embrace the new: the New Man, the resurrected Jesus and living our lives alive to God!

Before moving to the next chapter, here is a summary of what has been discussed in this chapter:

We started the chapter by a quote from Psalm 119 that speaks of Mercy as a kind of comfort that comes to us because of a "change" or a "reversing" that happens in our lives:

> *76 Let, I pray, your Merciful kindness be for my comfort, According to Your word to Your servant. [Psalm 119:76]*

The comfort referred to in scripture is related to the Flood of Noah. Noah, whose name means "comfort", was the man that was to bring "comfort" to all of mankind. This "comfort" was achieved through the washing away of every unrighteousness and, thereby, "reversing" the "curse" from "the land". This story was only pointing at what was to happen when Jesus would come. The "comfort" that comes to us through "His Mercy" is related to His suffering in "death", which would bring a "Flood": the shedding of His Blood. His blood, like a Flood, comes to mankind to cleanse all unrighteousness, evil and sin from his conscience. Thus Jesus, by rising from the dead, "reversed" the "curse" in the body of man for everyone. Whoever comes to Him to be baptized in His death will have his conscience cleansed from sin by His blood and, as a result, his body will be affected by coming out of this with a cleansed conscience (through the Flood of His blood): "resurrected into His new body". Through His resurrection, where the "curse is reversed", He "comforts" the soul of every man and brings them to "salvation".

Our cleansing of the conscience comes by "reckoning" ourselves as being dead to the body of sin (the old man). If we reckon ourselves to this fact (this truth), then we no longer listen to the voice of sin in our conscience but listen instead to the "voice of His blood" that has washed our conscience from sin. His Mercy comes like a Flood to remove us from our struggles, weaknesses, sicknesses and everything that is holding us back from the newness of life in Christ. Once His Mercy has washed us clean from the inside out, we then realize that His word is true: He is the God of "comfort"!

Mercy, The Voice of the Blood

The writer of the book of Hebrews writes, in the twelfth chapter, that we have come to the blood of Jesus Christ which speaks to us. We must heed the voice of this blood because it speaks better things than the voice of the blood of Abel:

> *22 But you have come to Mount Zion and to the city of the living God, the heavenly Jerusalem, to an innumerable company of angels, 23 to the general assembly and church of the firstborn [who are] registered in heaven, to God the Judge of all, to the spirits of just men made perfect, 24 to Jesus the Mediator of the new covenant, and to the blood of sprinkling that speaks better things than [that of] Abel. [Hebrews 12:22-24]*

We see from scripture that the blood of this new covenant has a "voice" and everyone who is under this new covenant must heed the voice of its blood. This blood speaks from a higher realm and authority than earth. It speaks from heaven; thus, the new covenant is of the heaven and is, therefore, heavenly.

We continue to read:

25 See that you do not refuse Him who speaks. For if they did not escape who refused him who spoke on earth, much more [shall we not escape] if we turn away from Him who [speaks] from heaven. [Hebrews 12:25]

This blood, as shown by Jesus in the last supper, is His blood that is shed for the remission of sin for everyone. His blood speaks from heaven and not from earth. In other words, it speaks from heaven on earth. It also speaks better things than the blood of Abel. The first account of the blood of Abel can be found in Genesis 4 after Cain killed him:

10 And He [the Lord] said, "What have you done? The voice of your brother's blood cries out to Me from the ground." [Genesis 4:10]

The blood of Abel was shed on earth and was speaking from earth after his brother, Cain, murdered him. The words "cries out" in the above verse are to be interpreted to mean "crying out for help in a situation that one cannot help himself". We see these words again in Psalm 17:

17 [The righteous] cry out, and the LORD hears and delivers them out of all their troubles. [Psalm 34:17]

The voice of the blood of righteous Abel began crying out to the Lord for help because his blood was shed on the ground. The earth, which earlier had been cursed because of Adam, had now become saturated with the blood of a righteous person. Here, Abel is crying out for help by asking the Lord to redeem him and deliver his blood from the earth, thus restoring his life back to him.

Hebrews 11 says that Abel was righteous because he offered a sacrifice that was acceptable to the Lord. The Lord accepted Abel's sacrifice, but He did not receive (accept) the offering of his brother Cain. What Abel offered was a better sacrifice; a true sacrifice that would come in Jesus Christ. This is why we read in Hebrews 11 that it is "by faith" that Abel offered a sacrifice acceptable to God so that he could have life. Through his sacrifice he was showing that the death of the true sacrifice would come in Jesus Christ and result in life for him:

4 By faith Abel offered to God a more excellent sacrifice than Cain, through which he obtained witness that he was righteous, God testifying of his gifts, and through it, he being dead still speaks. [Hebrews 11:4]

God accepted His sacrifice. Since the purpose of every sacrifice acceptable to the Lord is to redeem man from the curse and thus give him life. Abel's sacrifice was accounted to him for righteousness and life was Abel's portion because righteousness gives life[23].

Abel's sacrifice, however, was not pleasing to his brother, Cain; and even though Able was righteous he was still murdered by Cain and tasted death. His blood was shed on the ground and it started crying out for help to the Lord, reminding Him of the "accepted sacrifice" and thus asking for resurrection from the dead. Even though he died by the hand of his own brother, God still heard the voice of his blood. In other words, though Abel succumbed to death he continues to speak by way of his example: he asks for redemption and resurrection from the dead.

Abel symbolically represents Jesus: the righteous one whose sacrifice of His own body was accepted by God - yet He, too, was murdered by the hand of His own brothers. His blood was also shed on the ground and continues to speak, just as Abel's blood still speaks. However, His blood speaks better things which we are going to unveil shortly. This blood, which speaks, cries out for life and resurrection from the dead - not only for Himself but also for all those who come to Him and believe Him in His sacrifice:

7 Who, in the days of His flesh, when He had offered up prayers and supplications, with vehement cries and tears to Him who was able to save Him from death and was heard because of His godly fear. [Hebrews 5:7]

And,

[23] Galatians 3:21

8 Though He was a Son, [yet] He learned obedience by the things which He suffered. 9 And having been perfected, He became the author of eternal salvation to all who obey Him. [Hebrews 5:8-9]

During the night He was betrayed, and just before His crucifixion, Jesus was in a garden praying and submitting Himself to the will of the Father. It was the hour of weakness for Him; yet He resisted sin to bloodshed - to the point that His sweat became as drops of blood and fell on the ground before He was even scourged. The sweat of His face dropped on the same ground which was cursed by the sweat of Adam's face. His sweat was the blood He willingly shed for mankind. It was shed even for the ones who would crucify him and it was being shed even for all "Cains" in the world!

As previously mentioned, His blood that falls on the cursed ground reverses the curse; He later made this clear by saying: *"Father forgive them, they know not what they are doing"*[24]. Here He was saying to the Father that He was not going to ask for vengeance, but rather, forgiveness. By reversing the curse through forgiveness, man no longer has to live by the sweat of his own brow - which was the way of living inherited from Adam, but rather, in His comfort and righteousness.

Now let us find out what the voice of the blood says.

In Exodus 25, God explained to Moses how he was to build the Mercy Seat in the Most Holy place:

17 You shall make a Mercy Seat of pure gold; two and a half cubits [shall be] its length and a cubit and a half its width. 18 And you shall make two cherubim of gold; of hammered work, you shall make them at the two ends of the Mercy Seat. [Exodus 25:17-18]

And then He says:

21 You shall put the Mercy Seat on top of the ark, and in the ark, you shall put the Testimony that I will give you. [Exodus 25:21]

---

[24] Luke 23:34

God told Moses that He would give him the Testimony to put in the ark. Moses was also told to put the Mercy Seat on top of the ark and to make two Cherubim, with each one facing the Mercy Seat. Then the Lord said that He would speak with Moses from "above the Mercy Seat" and between the two Cherubim:

> *22 And there I will meet with you, and I will speak with you from above the Mercy Seat, from between the two cherubim which [are] on the ark of the Testimony, about everything which I will give you in commandment to the children of Israel. [Exodus 25:22]*

Next, Leviticus 16 gives the instruction for the "atonement for sin" and the role of Mercy Seat:

> *14 He shall take some of the blood of the bull and sprinkle [it] with his finger on the Mercy Seat on the east [side], and before the Mercy Seat he shall sprinkle some of the blood with his finger seven times. 15 Then he shall kill the goat of the sin offering, which [is] for the people, bring its blood inside the veil, do with that blood as he did with the blood of the bull, and sprinkle it on the Mercy Seat and before the Mercy Seat. [Leviticus 16:14-15]*

What we are to learn here is that after bringing the "sacrifice of sin offering" (the sacrificial animal), for the "atonement" (the forgiving/pardon of sin), the High Priest was required to take the blood of the sacrificial animal and sprinkle it on the Mercy Seat. Because we know that God said that He would speak "from above the Mercy Seat", here we are to see and understand that the voice that the Lord is referring to, is the voice of the "blood" that is on the Mercy Seat.

As mentioned earlier, the tabernacle of Moses and everything that God had shown Moses were only a shadow and a sign pointing at the true tabernacle which was to come. On the Mercy Seat, the blood of the sacrificial animal (for example, a goat or lamb) for the sin offering would become the blood of Jesus, which was shed for removal (atonement) of sin. The blood of animals was shed on the Mercy Seat, but the blood of Jesus is shed in heavenly places; it was not for the cleansing of dirt from mankind's flesh, but rather, to cleanse mankind's conscience from sin.

> *11 But Christ came [as] High Priest of the good things to come, with the greater and more perfect tabernacle not made with hands, that is, not of this creation. 12 Not with the blood of goats and calves, but with His own blood He entered the Most Holy Place once for all, having obtained eternal redemption. 13 For if the blood of bulls and goats and the ashes of a heifer, sprinkling the unclean, sanctifies for the purifying of the flesh, 14 how much more shall the blood of Christ, who through the eternal Spirit offered Himself without spot to God, cleanse your conscience from dead works to serve the living God? [Hebrews 9:11-14]*

In the old, blood was shed on the Mercy Seat from which God spoke. In the new, the blood of Jesus is shed on the conscience. Thus, the Mercy Seat in the old was pointing at the conscience of people in the new because that is where God resides and where He speaks from into our hearts.

Our conscience is the Mercy Seat of God, and it is where He speaks from to us. Because the sacrificial blood was always shed on the Mercy Seat, we are to understand that the blood of Jesus is shed on our conscience (the New Mercy Seat) and thus, speaks "Mercy" to us!

This voice of God, however, can be heard only when the blood is shed to cleanse our conscience from sin; that is when His voice is heard in our heart. The blood that speaks is a "Testimony" that God has accepted the sacrifice and because the sacrifice is accepted we can receive what the sacrifice was killed and offered for. The voice of God constantly speaks Mercy into our hearts, so that we come to understand that we are no longer bound to our mistakes and their consequences. Instead, the blood is shed to cleanse our conscience from sin, errors and mistakes and to bring Mercy to us instead of accusation, judgment and condemnation.

Paul writes in Romans 6 that we should not obey sin any longer:

> *12 Therefore do not let sin reign in your mortal body, that you should obey it in its lusts. [Romans 6:12]*

Through the blood of Jesus, we have been freed from sin. Our conscience, which was the throne of sin, from which sin reigned and ruled over us, is now and forever cleansed by the blood of Jesus. Therefore, all we need to do is to obey the voice of the blood that we hear and not to obey the voice of sin. It is about two voices: Sin and the Blood!

The meaning of the word "obey" in the original language is "listening" or "heading" to a voice. For instance, if you hear someone knocking at the door and you respond by getting up to go open the door, you are actually obeying the voice you heard within yourself. Paul likens sin to someone knocking on the door; the way it knocks is through the voice that it speaks. We will not obey sin if we do not respond to its voice.

In Genesis 4, God came to Cain right before he murdered his brother and told him:

> *7 "If you do well, will you not be accepted? And if you do not do well, sin lies at the door. And its desire [is] for you, but you should rule over it." [Genesis 4:7]*

More or less what God was telling Cain was that sin was knocking at the door of his conscience, but that he was not to obey its voice (meaning, he was not to open the door). This is how Cain would be able to rule over sin. But we now know that Cain instead opened the door to sin and was ultimately ruled by it.

What is evident from these scriptures is that sin has a voice that can reach to man's conscience. Thus, man's conscience is a door that sin knocks on in order to enter and is a place that sin will dwell in it if allowed in. Regrettably, many have obeyed, listened or heeded to this voice of sin by opening the door of their conscience and, as the result, allowed death to come into their lives. Death reigns through sin! But sin and its voice will leave the conscience when someone more powerful and stronger than sin comes in (i.e. the blood of Jesus), binds it up, takes its armour away, splits it apart, overcomes it and cleanses the conscience from what was occupying it:

> *21 When a strong man, fully armed, guards his own palace, his goods are in peace. 22 But when a stronger than he comes upon him and overcomes him, he takes from him all his armor in which he trusted and divides his spoils. 23 He who is not with Me is against Me, and he who does not gather with Me scatters. [Luke 11:21-23]*

The blood of Jesus as "the stronger man", enters the house of our conscience, comes upon the "strong man" (sin), binds him and overcomes him. This blood takes away from sin all its armour in which it trusted and splits it apart. Thus, His blood takes the place of sin and sits in the conscience to reign over sin and destroy it completely by wiping it away from our conscience of people. It is then our hearts begin hearing another voice (the voice of His blood), which is contrary to the voice of sin. The voice of His blood melts the voice of sin in our hearts, allowing us to live according to His Mercy.

A clear conscience causes the heart to hear a voice that results in either faith or unbelief; obedience or disobedience.

> *22 let us draw near with a true heart in full assurance of faith, having our hearts sprinkled from an evil conscience and our bodies washed with pure water. [Hebrews 10:22]*

If the Bible says "the heart must be cleansed from an evil conscience", then conscience is in the heart and that is where a voice can be heard. This is why we read:

> *15 While it is said: "Today if you will hear His voice, do not harden your <u>hearts</u> as in the rebellion." [Hebrews 3:15]*

Our conscience is the door upon which both sin and the blood of Jesus can knock. The first brings punishment; the second brings Mercy. One gives us a knowledge of good and evil; the other gives us the knowledge of the death of Jesus. The first brings death; the other brings life.

The literal meaning of "sin" is "missing the mark" or "falling short of perfection". If we translate this concept into daily examples, sin becomes the voice that tells us how much we have missed or failed; how weak we are; how unworthy we are; and how imperfect and guilty we are. It is a voice that tries to focus our attention on ourselves and our weaknesses. Through believing this voice, we make certain decisions and take certain actions. For example, if we look at the story of Eve in Genesis 3, we will realize that what caused her to eat of the fruit was the weakness she saw in herself. She then tried to "fix it"; so, she thought the fruit of the tree could add something to her that she was lacking:

> *6 So when the woman saw that the tree [was] good for food, that it [was] pleasant to the eyes, and a tree desirable to make [one] wise, she took of its fruit and ate. She also gave to her husband with her, and he ate. [Genesis 3:6]*

Eve desired to be wise because, through her conversation with the serpent, she presumed that she was not wise; she had unknowingly been deceived. Had she believed that she "was" wise, she would not have thought that she needed to "become" wise. There is nothing wrong with wanting to be wise, but the problem, in this case, was that her desire to be wise came about from the "lack" she saw in herself. In "obedience" to the serpent's voice - the voice that deceptively told her she lacked wisdom - Eve mistakenly decided to resolve her lack of wisdom by using the "solution" provided to her by the serpent and not by God. Eve's obedience to the serpent's voice caused her to become serpent's slave. Not only did she not become wise; her eyes were opened to herself and she saw that she was naked. Fear suddenly overcame and gripped her, as well as Adam, and they became slaves to their fear.

The reason fear reigns in the life of man is that by listening to the voice of sin, man becomes self-focused and self-conscience. Once his eyes are opened to himself, all he sees is weakness of the flesh. Because he thinks he must resolve this issue by himself, he becomes afraid. Thus, when Eve saw herself naked, she became afraid. She covered herself with the fig leaves, thinking that the fig leaves would remove her fear. But what she did not know was that the fig leaves would soon wither and, once again, she would see the shame of her nakedness, leaving her to remain in a state of perpetual fear:

> *7 Then the eyes of both of them were opened, and they knew that they [were] naked; and they sewed fig leaves together and made themselves coverings. [Genesis 3:7]*

Adam and Eve's eyes were opened when they had both eaten from the fruit of the same tree (the fig tree). Because both of them were standing by the same fig tree, they used the leaves of the same tree to cover the nakedness (the "lack") that they saw. Here we are to understand that the tree of the Knowledge of Good and Evil, which is symbolic of sin, first opens the eyes of man to his own weakness, then it offers him a solution to "cover up" the lack rather than resolving it; it brings a temporary solution, not a permanent one. That is why man remains in constant fear until a permanent solution is provided through his hearing of another voice: "the voice of the blood" - "the Mercy". This voice enters man's conscience, offering him to eat of the fruit of the Tree of Life so that his eyes can be opened to the power of God. In doing so, man puts on the leaves of the Tree of Life and is thereby set free from fear.

> *14 But put on the Lord Jesus Christ, and make no provision for the flesh, to [fulfill its] lusts. [Romans 13:14]*

The fig tree or the tree of Knowledge of Good and Evil must be left to dry up from the root so that the Tree of Life can grow, multiply and bear much fruit for man. It is for this reason that Jesus, on the way to Jerusalem right before His crucifixion, cursed a fig tree and the fig tree withered immediately:

> *13 And seeing from afar a fig tree having leaves, He went to see if perhaps He would find something on it. When He came to it, He found nothing but leaves, for it was not the season for figs. 14 In response, Jesus said to it, "<u>Let no one eat fruit from you ever again</u>." And His disciples heard [it]. [Mark 11:13-14]*

The gospel of Matthew shows that Jesus said to the fig tree "let no fruit grow on you ever again":

> *19 And seeing a fig tree by the road, He came to it and found nothing on it but leaves, and said to it, "Let no fruit grow on you ever again." Immediately the fig tree withered away. [Matthew 21:19]*

By this statement, Jesus not only declares that no one will eat of its fruit, but He is also declaring that the tree itself will never bear fruit because it will wither from the face of the ground. By this, Jesus prophetically put an end to the fruit-bearing season of the fig tree. This tree, symbolically, was the tree that many ate of and died, beginning with Adam and Eve in the garden of Eden. Jesus put an end to the fruit-bearing season of this tree because He would soon to be crucified and through His death, many would have life - the time had come for the Tree of Life (Jesus), to bear fruit so that many may eat of it, clothe themselves with Him and have life!

Paul says in Galatians:

> *13 Christ has redeemed us from the curse of the law, having become a curse for us (for it is written, "Cursed [is] everyone who hangs on a tree"). [Galatians 3:13]*

And,

> *14 That the blessing of Abraham might come upon the Gentiles in Christ Jesus, that we might receive the promise of the Spirit through faith. [Galatians 3:14]*

When Jesus was hung on the cross, as scripture tells us above, He became a "curse" so that "curse" could be taken away from us and the "blessing" which was promised to Abraham would come upon us. Jesus, hanging on the cross, fulfilled the prophecy of the old saying: *"Cursed is the one who hangs on a tree"*[25].

Jesus cursed the fig tree and it withered. Perhaps a few days later, this same withered tree became His own cross, carried to Golgotha,

[25] Galatian 3:10

where He was crucified. He became that cursed fig tree, taking upon Himself the curse of mankind and by dying as the cursed one, He "nailed" the curse to the cross, thus the tree or the curse withered. When He was raised from the dead, He was raised a New Man - the firstborn from the dead who has overcome death for all mankind. He has brought many to this "Perfect Man" - a Man who is not bound to sin and death but, instead, is free from them.

Jesus shed His blood and caused the withering of the cursed tree through His own death so that when man comes to this tree to eat from its fruit, may see the blood on it as a testimony speaking:

"This is the end of death, I shed my soul, my blood, on this tree in your place, now look for life, for another tree".

The blood on this withered tree is a sign that points to another tree which is always green - the "Tree of Life", from which we may eat of its fruit and clothe ourselves with its leaves and live. By contrast, the "tree of the Knowledge of Good and Evil" in the garden, in Genesis, was never for mankind. Mankind was never supposed to eat of it nor die. Instead, mankind was only supposed to see the death of the Son of God and realize that life is his portion. The tree of the Knowledge of Good and Evil was only to be used as a sign to show the pathway to the Tree of Life so that mankind could find it, eat of its fruit and live.

The questions that usually come up when we talk about how Jesus put an end to sin and death is this: "If Jesus has done this, why then is it that people still die?", or, "Why is it that people still sin?". The answer to these questions is quite simple: There is a difference between what Jesus has accomplished and finished, compared to what we can (and are to) receive from Him through our belief in Him. This is why the preaching of the gospel is essential to us. Once we know what He has done and what He has accomplished, we can then receive it by believing. If He had not removed the power of sin from us, we could never live free. We are able to begin living in the freedom He has provided for us, once we know that He has broken the power of sin over us and has set us free from all the bondage.

Regrettably, people are still eating from the "tree of the knowledge of Good and Evil" and die from doing so - even though this tree has already dried up from the root. Thankfully, through the preaching of the gospel, God reveals to us that He has put an end to this tree and there is another tree that man can eat of. The way to this tree - the Tree of Life - is open to all mankind. Mankind can be led by the voice of the blood of Jesus to this tree and eat of it. Yet even though God has done all of this for mankind, it remains up to mankind to choose to follow the voice of God, allow his or her heart know about what He has done, believe in that, become free from the bondages that he or she still carries and, by doing so, be led to the tree that is always green and bears fruit to eternal life.

In the next chapter, we will discuss the truth regarding these trees as being "planted" in the heart of man. Because the heart of man is the "field" or, in other words, the "ground" in which a tree is rooted. Before moving to the next chapter, however, I will briefly summarize some of the key points that were covered in this chapter.

The blood of Jesus shed for us on the tree of Knowledge of Good and Evil (which was planted in our hearts), causes the tree to wither. This blood cries out in our conscience for Mercy, so that our eyes can be opened to see the power of God. Mercy causes us to lift up our eyes from ourselves - from our weaknesses and lack and, instead, places our focus on His power. Through this power we receive His solution and provision for our lives; a permanent solution that never fades away, unlike the leaves of the fig tree that wither away.

The voice of the blood brings us to a place of receiving His love, thus causing us to trust Him and receive His covering for us from the leaves of the Tree of Life, which is His own body. His blood, which cries out Mercy for us, brings a conviction of His power into our hearts and offers us His body to put on and be clothed with. He does this for us so that we never become slaves of fear but, instead, become bound to His Love; never hiding behind our works, but running to Him in full assurance of heart, knowing that His Mercy is His power shown to the weak and helpless when it is needed.

Mercy, Our Food

We have been looking at different aspects of Mercy in the previous chapters. Even though I am closing the book with this chapter, I feel as though we have only just scratched the surface of what Mercy really is. I pray for all of us that in the coming days, weeks and years, God may reveal to all of us even a greater depth of this powerful attribute of the loving God.

When Moses made the covenant with people, he dedicated it with blood. Scripture tells us how he did this:

> *18 Therefore not even the first [covenant] was dedicated without blood. 19 For when Moses had spoken every precept to all the people according to the law, he took the blood of calves and goats, with water, scarlet wool, and hyssop, and sprinkled both the book itself and all the people, 20 saying, "This [is] the blood of the covenant which God has commanded you." 21 Then likewise he sprinkled with blood both the tabernacle and all the vessels of the ministry. 22 And according to the law, almost all things are purified with blood, and without shedding of blood, there is no remission. [Hebrews 9:18-22]*

This verse tells us that purification was always done through the "sprinkling of the blood". Under the old covenant, it is important to point out that this manner of purification (cleansing) was only done externally, on the flesh, as explained in verse 13 of the same chapter:

13 For if the blood of bulls and goats and the ashes of a heifer, sprinkling the unclean, sanctifies for the purifying of the flesh. [Hebrews 9:13]

Every manner of purification (cleansing) under the old covenant was performed according to the law, which was a set of "fleshly" commandments. For this reason, such purification was powerless to cleanse the "inside" of man, or in other words, man's "conscience".

Under the new covenant, however, the blood of Jesus has the power to cleanse man's conscience, because He offered His own blood, once for all, for the removal of sin. If sin is cleansed once and for all, there is no need for further cleansing. This also means that there is no requirement of any sort of offering for the removing of sin and, hence, there is no remembrance of sin anymore. As a result, man's conscience is no longer affected by sin and, for this reason, it remains clean.

Under the old covenant, the children of Israel were required to bring forward sacrifices for their sin each year. This repetitive ritual of offering sacrifices served as a constant reminder to them of their sin. Therefore, their conscience was always aware of sin and not cleansed from it.

13 For if the blood of bulls and goats and the ashes of a heifer, sprinkling the unclean, sanctifies for the purifying of the flesh, 14 how much more shall the blood of Christ, who through the eternal Spirit offered Himself without spot to God, cleanse your conscience from dead works to serve the living God? [Hebrews 9:13-14]

And,

1 For the law, having a shadow of the good things to come, [and] not the very image of the things, can never with these same sacrifices, which they offer continually year by year, make those who approach perfect. 2 For then would they not have ceased to be offered? For the worshipers, once purified, would have had no more consciousness of sins. 3 But in those [sacrifices there is] a reminder of sins every year. 4 For [it is] not possible that the blood of bulls and goats could take away sins. [Hebrews 10:1-4]

Just as we have seen before and also as confirmed in the above verses, the issue of sin is internal; it is embedded within the conscience of people. Before sin manifests itself externally through words, behaviours or actions in the flesh, it is rooted in conscience. That is why the blood of the sacrificed animals could never take away sin.

As long as people continued to bring forward a sacrifice for the forgiveness of sin, they continued to remember their sin. That is why no sacrifice could ever remove sin from them - except One. The remembrance of sin compelled man to repeatedly bring forward sacrifices, over and over again. In doing so, man became trapped in a vicious cycle of repeatedly offering sacrifices that could never take his sin away.

It is not only sin that must be removed from mankind but also the remembrance of sin from his conscience. This is the only way that mankind is delivered from sin and safeguarded from committing an act of sin; this is what the blood of Jesus does for mankind!

Certainly, I am not suggesting that one should be oblivious of sin while being ruled by it. A person who is the slave of sin and yet says that he does not sin is typically the one who also says he does not need the blood of Jesus to remove his sin and cleanse the conscience. What I am trying to convey here is that we need the blood of Jesus to cleanse our conscience to such a level that it matures us to the perfection of the "Perfect Man". This is where the conscience is without blemish and we can freely walk in the perfection of "Christ in us". As long as the conscience is polluted by sin, man continues to live in sin and, hence, is in need of the blood of Jesus. Not that He needs to be sacrificed again, but that we may remember the communion of His blood.

Because sin in the conscience could not be taken away through the blood of sacrificed animals, it could never make anyone perfect. In other words, a conscience that still remembers sin is not a conscience of perfection or a perfect conscience; rather, it is a conscience of sin.

9 It [was] symbolic for the present time in which both gifts and sacrifices are offered which cannot make him who performed the service perfect in regard to the conscience. [Hebrews 9:9]

God is calling us to "move on to perfection", eating of the "solid food" which belongs to the mature and perfect sons of God:

12 For though by this time you ought to be teachers, you need [someone] to teach you again the first principles of the oracles of God; and you have come to need milk and not solid food. 13 For everyone who partakes [only] of milk [is] unskilled in the word of righteousness, for he is a babe. 14 But solid food belongs to those who are of full age (Perfect), [that is], those who by reason of use have their senses exercised to discern both good and evil. [Hebrews 5:12-14]

The words "full age" in verse 14 are the same exact words used in Hebrews 9:9 and mean "perfect". According to the above verses, the ones who are "perfect" are the ones that have come to eat "solid food". In other words, they have passed the period of "drinking milk" which is not a solid food. Verse 13 says that the one who still drinks the milk and not the solid food is unskilled in the "word of righteousness". We can then say that this "word of righteousness" is the solid food for the perfect ones!

If "perfection" is in regards to "conscience" and the "word of righteousness" is a solid food for the "perfect ones", then this particular solid food is for man's conscience. It is not ordinary food that one ingests into one's stomach. To be more precise, the Word of righteousness is "the" food that feeds the inner part of man.

9 Do not be carried about with various and strange doctrines. For [it is] good that the heart be established by grace, not with foods which have not profited those who have been occupied with them. [Hebrews 13:9]

Looking closely at this verse, we do not feed our heart with food, but rather, our stomach. With this in mind, the food that this verse is referring to is not that of "ordinary food" that is ingested by man for sustenance purposes. Here the word "food" refers to various and strange "doctrines" or, in other words, "teachings". This verse tells us that such doctrines or teachings, when obeyed by man, do not make man stronger deep within himself (within his "inner man"). Because, quite simply, they are contrary to "grace" - which is what we are to use to feed our hearts with. In other words, we are to feed our heart with the "true doctrine", which is grace.

The feeding of our heart comes through our conscience:

> *22 Let us draw near with a true heart in full assurance of faith, having our hearts sprinkled from an evil conscience and our bodies washed with pure water. [Hebrews 10:22]*

In essence, these verses are telling us that the heart of a person will be cleansed when their conscience is first cleansed. A true heart is a heart that is in full assurance of faith; it is a heart that is clean. This cleansing of the heart happens by the cleansing of the conscience from "evil", as is indicated in this verse. In previous chapters, we also discussed that the conscience must be cleansed from "sin" and "dead works" as well. We can see then that "sin", "dead works" and "evil" are in the same category and they all must be removed from conscience. Once the conscience is clear from these, then the heart is clear from them as well and, therefore, faith rises up. As long as sin, evil and dead works reside in one's conscience, faith has no place to reside in one's heart.

That is why Hebrews 3 says:

> *12 Beware, brethren, lest there be in any of you an evil heart of unbelief in departing from the living God. [Hebrews 3:12]*

According to this verse, the "evil heart" is a "heart of unbelief". Simply stated, evil is unbelief.

We read in Hebrews 10:22 that we need to have our hearts detached from an "evil conscience". The evil of unbelief in the heart happens because of the unbelief in the conscience. Faith and unbelief "coincide" together in the heart, but they are both "influenced" from the conscience. In other words, when the conscience is cleansed from unbelief, the heart is able to hold faith within it.

By far, we have seen that sin dwells in the conscience and blood sprinkles the conscience as well. Sin, in the conscience, speaks to people convincing them to do certain works which are called "dead works" - actions that produce death! On the other hand, the blood of Jesus also speaks to people in their conscience, convincing them of the Mercy of God so that they do not need to be bound to sin and obey its voice; they can obey the voice of Mercy and have life.

The voice of sin in the conscience causes the heart to be filled with unbelief. Likewise, the voice of the blood (which is Mercy) cleanses the conscience from unbelief and fills the heart with faith.

> *17 So then faith [comes] by hearing, and hearing by the word of God. [Romans 10:17]*

Faith comes by hearing. But does it come by hearing of the ears? No! Many can hear the same message with their ears, but only some will believe it. This verse speaks of a hearing in the heart. It is through the conscience in the heart where faith dwells. Therefore, hearing the word of God through the conscience causes evil, sin and dead works to be wiped away from the heart and allows faith to rise up instead.

In a previous chapter, we mentioned that the Lord told Moses that He would speak to him from above the Mercy Seat, where the blood was shed. Therefore, what the word of God speaks to our heart through the conscience is according to His Mercy; it is not according to accusations, judgment or condemnation or death. The latter is the voice of sin, not the voice of the blood!

The moment our heart hears a voice that is according to the Mercy of God, faith rises up. That is why we read in multiple places in the New Testament that "*The just shall live by faith*":

> *38 Now the just shall live by faith; But if [anyone] draws back, my soul has no pleasure in him. [Hebrews 10:38]*

The word "just" in the New Testament is to be interpreted by its readers to mean someone who constantly lives by hearing the "word" of God - the "voice" of the blood that speaks "Mercy" into his heart, causing it to be filled with faith. The "just" does not listen to the voice of sin which, as we have previously discussed, serves only to reveal a "lack". This voice offers a solution(s) to cover up this lack and can cause one to do something to attain what is lacking. In doing so, one ultimately falls into unbelief. This is exactly what happened to Adam and Eve when they ate from the tree that God had told them not to:

> *6 So when the woman saw that the tree [was] good for food, that it [was] pleasant to the eyes, and a tree desirable to make [one] wise, she took of its fruit and ate. She also gave to her husband with her, and he ate. [Genesis 3:6]*

Eve saw that the tree was "good for food" and could "make her wise" and that is why she ate its fruit. She did not eat the "evil", she ate the "good" and that is what brought death upon her. It was not the "evil" that killed Adam and Eve, it was the "good"! This means that even the "good" from the wrong tree is evil and brings death.

What was wrong with Eve's desire to be wise? I touched on this question briefly in the last chapter and will elaborate on it further here. The reason Eve desired to be wise was that she first acknowledged she was not! She saw a lack within herself and believed that she did not have something that she thought she ought to have. In doing so, she then desired what she thought she lacked. Through her conversation with the serpent in the garden, she was deceived and believed a lie – which was that God had not given her wisdom. In believing this lie, she began looking for wisdom from a different source. But through this process, not only did Eve not become wise, but she also became foolish and exchanged the wisdom of God with her own foolishness. When she (and Adam) saw their own nakedness (to them, another lack and weakness), they became afraid and immediately looked for a solution to cover their new found "lack", as well. By way of their own wisdom, they chose to wear fig leaves from the tree to cover their bodies - even though they were supposed to be "covered" by God Himself, as Romans 13 says:

> *14 But put on the Lord Jesus Christ, and make no provision for the flesh, to [fulfill its] lusts. [Romans 13:14]*

It is foolishness to look for wisdom from a different source other than God. Man was made to be in union and fellowship with God because he was made in the likeness of God. Mankind was created to walk with God, live in a love relationship with Him and to be convinced of God's love. Through this walk, mankind was to be guided by God; to eat of the fruit of the Tree of Life and continue to live with God. Man was also made to rule and reign on earth through communion and oneness with God, not by trying to overcome things with his own wisdom, his own coverings and his own plans. Mankind's ways and solutions are always temporary; they are akin to putting on fig leaves, which soon will wither!

The interesting part is that before eating of the forbidden tree which caused Adam and Eve to see their nakedness, they were naked but they were not ashamed:

> *25 And they were both naked, the man and his wife, and were not ashamed. [Genesis 2:25]*

They were naked from the beginning! It is not that they were not naked and later became so by eating! No! They were naked, but their eyes were not open to their nakedness. By blindness to the shame of nakedness, they were supposed to heed the voice of God and find the Tree of Life; they were to eat from that tree and be covered by its leaves. However, and as we have learned, once they ate from the forbidden tree, not only did they not listen to the voice of God, they hid themselves from God behind the fig leaves they had covered themselves with. So how could they now follow God's voice to find the Tree of Life while they were scared of Him and hiding themselves from life?

Sin had entered their conscience. Their hearts became dark and their minds void of truth. Sadly, this story holds true even to this day for everyone born of Adam. Mankind has exchanged the glory of the incorruptible God, with the glory of corruptible man:

> *21 Because, although they knew God, they did not glorify [Him] as God, nor were thankful, but became futile in their thoughts, and their foolish hearts were darkened. 22 Professing to be wise, they became fools, 23 and changed the glory of the incorruptible God into an image made like corruptible man and birds and four-footed animals and creeping things. [Romans 1:21-23]*

Thankfully, however, God never changed His mind. His plan for mankind is still the same: "to eat from the Tree of Life". But in order for man to eat from it, he must find the tree by hearing the voice of God, trusting and following Him toward the tree.

In order for man to believe in God and to follow Him to the Tree of Life, man's conscience first needs to be cleansed from sin. When this happens, man does not hide from God anymore and does not count himself worthy of punishment and death anymore. On the contrary, man embraces God; he runs to him and through the process of eating from the food that God gives him, he will have eternal life.

From the beginning of time, it has always been about food and eating. As we have learned, the tree that Adam and Eve ate from, which eventually caused death to come about, was called the: "tree of the Knowledge of Good and Evil". If we look at this tree in the literal sense and not symbolically, we see that we are unable to find a tree or a fruit by this name for purchase. On the other hand, just as I had mentioned in a previous chapter, this tree is the fig tree. But we eat figs just as we do any other fruit, but nothing similar to what happened to Adam and Eve happens to us. If or when we eat figs, our eyes do not open to see our nakedness, nor do we hide ourselves somewhere or become afraid. In fact, one may die and have never eaten figs! My point here is that this particular tree – The tree of the Knowledge of Good and Evil – would not have been a natural tree that bears fruits to feed the stomach. It was a tree that had symbolic significance used by God to illustrate to us what happens in the heart and conscience of man. Let us next look at this a little deeper.

Jesus often compared man to a tree. In response to the Pharisees, the teachers of the law, He said:

> *33 Either make the tree good and its fruit good, or else make the tree bad and its fruit bad; for a tree is known by [its] fruit. 34 Brood of vipers! How can you, being evil, speak good things? For out of the abundance of the heart the mouth speaks. [Matthew 12:33-34]*

Here Jesus is speaking about this truth: *"every tree produces fruits after its own kind"*. In other words, the type of a tree defines what kind of fruit one should expect to receive from it. Case in point - the fig tree cannot produce grapes, nor can a grapevine produce figs.

He further adds to this by saying that *"only a good tree can produce good fruit"*. We cannot expect to have good fruit from a bad tree. Jesus continues further on by saying to the teachers of the law: *"how can you speak good things when you are evil"*. By this, He is comparing "being evil" to a "tree" (a bad tree) and "speaking good" to the "fruit of the tree" (good fruit). Therefore, the "tree" symbolically refers to a "man" and the "fruits" of the tree are the "words" of a man.

Jesus also tells us: *"out of the abundance of the heart the mouth speaks"*- meaning that if "spoken words" from one's mouth are the "fruits" of the tree, then the "heart" must be the "tree". A better and more accurate interpretation is simply this: the tree that is planted grows in the heart and bears its fruit on the lips.

When God shaped creation, He said that *"every seed will produce after its own kind, and the seed of every fruit will be in itself"*. Because of this truth, when a fruit is eaten, its seed (which is in the fruit) is also eaten and it will further produce after its own kind.

For the same reason, when Adam and Eve ate from the fruit of the tree of the Knowledge of Good and Evil, the seed of the fruit they ate fell on the ground of their hearts and began producing more fruit after its own kind. That is why after Eve ate the fruit, it was she herself who then went to Adam and gave him the fruit to eat; it was not the serpent, it was Eve!

> *6 So when the woman saw that the tree [was] good for food, that it [was] pleasant to the eyes, and a tree desirable to make [one] wise, she took of its fruit and ate. She also gave to her husband with her, and he ate. [Genesis 3:6]*

Here we are to see that Eve had now become the tree! And because she was now the tree, she bore its fruit and someone else was now also eating of her fruit – her husband, Adam.

Let us bear in mind that Hebrews 13 urges us to not occupy ourselves with strange doctrine, but rather, to feed our hearts with grace:

> *9 Do not be carried about with various and strange doctrines. For [it is] good that the heart be established by grace, not with foods which have not profited those who have been occupied with them. [Hebrews 13:9]*

For additional clarity, let us now briefly summarize what has been discussed thus far. If a doctrine (teaching) is food (fruit) for someone's heart, then, the fruit of the tree of the Knowledge of Good and Evil was simply a kind of "knowledge", a "doctrine". What Adam and Eve ate was a knowledge or a doctrine that they had heard from the serpent. That doctrine grew in each of their hearts like a tree - filling their hearts and allowing no room for true knowledge – thus rendering hearts that were completely filled with unbelief. Throughout this process, their hearts became dark, full of evil (unbelief) and out of the abundance of that, they began to speak the words of the wisdom of the serpent! This is the mechanism by which the serpent multiplied itself and also why that same serpent of old is seen in the book of Revelation as a Dragon![26]

Now let us find out how one can eat from the fruit of a tree, a doctrine or even a knowledge. This is what God told Adam after he ate from the wrong tree:

---

[26] Revelation 12:9

> *17 Then to Adam He said, "Because you have heeded the voice of your wife and have eaten from the tree of which I commanded you, saying, 'You shall not eat of it'; Cursed [is] the ground for your sake; In toil you shall eat [of] it All the days of your life." [Genesis 3:17]*

As we have learned in this chapter thus far, it was not the serpent that came to Adam offering him the fruit; it was his own wife. Eve gave the fruit to her husband by speaking to him about what she thought she knew (a knowledge) from within her heart; a knowledge that she had gained from the serpent and was passing down to her husband. She was now a tree in her heart; its fruits were growing as words on her lips and, in speaking to Adam, she was offering him her fruits. Her words were the fruit of the tree of the Knowledge of Good and Evil, yet Adam ate of it by heeding her voice.

In a symbolic fashion, the eating of the fruit of a tree is in the heeding of words that we hear. In other words, by believing the words of a doctrine or a knowledge that we hear, we eat of that doctrine or knowledge!

We can now see how the serpent taught Eve and Eve taught her husband. The fruit of one provided seed for another, which was the planting of the same tree in those who received it. This is how the "multiplication and increasing" happened, which continued to such a level that the whole earth became full of trees of the Knowledge of Good and Evil. This is also how sin was spread to all mankind and polluted the conscience of man –through the voice of foolish reasonings that man heard and obeyed. As a consequence, death began to reign over mankind through sin and was now sitting on the throne of the authority of man: "his conscience".

The voice that we hear through the conscience is the food in our hearts. Mankind has been eating from a fruit that has brought him death since the time of creation, even though man was supposed to be eating of food that would instead give him life. Since the fruit that brought death was only a knowledge or a doctrine, likewise the food that brings life is also a knowledge or a doctrine.

In the previous chapter, we had a detailed study of the blood of Jesus. We saw that the blood of Jesus has a voice which has the power to cleanse man's conscience from the voice of sin. The voice of the blood cries out "Mercy" in the conscience of man. This voice provides food for man in his heart; food that man can eat and drink, by believing and heeding this voice. In doing so, he will not eat from a kind of fruit that will minister death to him but, instead, will eat from the fruit that brings him life: Mercy.

Jesus made some strong statements in the gospel of John, but more specifically in chapter 6:

> *53 Then Jesus said to them, "Most assuredly, I say to you, unless you eat the flesh of the Son of Man and drink His blood, you have no life in you.*
>
> *54 Whoever eats My flesh and drinks My blood has eternal life, and I will raise him up at the last day.*
>
> *55 For My flesh is food indeed, and My blood is drink indeed.*
>
> *56 He who eats My flesh and drinks My blood abides in Me, and I in him.*
>
> *57 As the living Father sent Me, and I live because of the Father, so he who feeds on Me will live because of Me." [John 6:53-57]*

But before that He said:

> *47 Most assuredly, I say to you, he who believes in Me has everlasting life. [John 6:47]*

On one hand, He says: *"if you believe in me you have everlasting life"*; on the other hand, He says: *"if you eat of my flesh and drink of my blood you have everlasting life"*. By putting these verses together, we can see again that "eating of His flesh and drinking of His blood" is by "believing" in what He has done for us, which is the breaking of His body and the shedding of His blood on the cross. In believing what He has done for us on the cross, we eat from His body and His blood. It is only through our believing that we feed ourselves - not our stomach, but rather, our conscience and heart. By this, we have life because we are eating from a food which gives life.

However, a few verses later and after many were offended at Him because of His words and left Him, He turned to His disciples saying:

> *63 It is the Spirit who gives life; the flesh profits nothing. The words that I speak to you are spirit, and [they] are life. [John 6:63]*

In this verse, Jesus clarifies that life is in His words because His "words" are "Spirit and Life". With that said, we also know that He has said that life comes from the eating and drinking of His flesh and the blood.

Let us next see how we are to reconcile both these teachings together. The words of Jesus reveal and make known a "knowledge" which is about "His flesh and blood". The one who "hears" this knowledge and "believes" it will have everlasting life, for it is this knowledge that brings "life" to mankind. What He has done for mankind on the cross is also a knowledge, and it is revealed to mankind through the Spirit by His word. Once we "hear" and "believe" this knowledge (or, doctrine), we are eating the fruit of the tree of life that brings life to us. In other words, life for mankind comes from the death of Jesus. Our life is dependent on His death and it is only because of His death that we can have life.

Even though we know that Jesus died for all that they may have life, not all have life; not even in His church. In the Book of Revelation, Jesus writes to one of the seven churches encouraging them to "overcome" and then "eat from the Tree of Life"[27]. This supports the fact that even in today's day and age there are churches in existence that do not eat from the Tree of Life, even though Jesus died that they too may have life.

All of this shows us two things about eating from the Tree of Life. First, that if we do not have the *revelation knowledge* of His work on the cross, and second, if we do not *believe it*, then we are not *eating*

---

[27] Revelation 3:1-6

from the Tree of Life. This suggests that there is a high probability that we still remain under the fig tree - the tree of the Knowledge of Good and Evil - feeding ourselves with food that does not bring us life! Simply stated, what Jesus has done for mankind through His crucifixion is either not revealed to us (because we are not hearing the voice of the Spirit) or we do not yet believe it, that is why some of us still eat from a wrong tree. But when we intentionally incline our ears to listen, with focus, to what the Spirit is saying (revealing) to us about His Mercy and grace (just as Jesus was exhorting all seven churches in the book of Revelation to do), we are able to "overcome" unbelief.

Heeding the voice of the Spirit reveals to us the Mercy of His blood and the grace of His body. This is what feeds our conscience with life-giving food: Mercy and grace. When the voice of the Spirit reveals God's Mercy and grace to us, our heart is cleansed from unbelief, so that we can believe Him for life.

That which the Spirit reveals in our heart is and will always be in accordance with the grace and Mercy of what His body and blood accomplished for us on the cross. If we continue to heed the Spirit's voice daily, we feed our heart with these foods, and our heart becomes strengthened and established by this. Because we eat of these fruits, their seeds plant a tree in our heart that then continues to produce the same good fruits from which many others will eat of and live. This is the mechanism by which the earth will be filled with life (the glory of God).

Jesus, by the grace of God, tasted death for everyone. His body was broken and ripped open and His blood was poured out. Through His broken body (His grace), His blood (His Mercy) pours out like a Flood; feeding every dry land, covering every hiding place and shedding forth light into every darkness from within Himself, so that we can once again become a well-watered garden, where the Tree of Life dwells. We are invited and called to rest under this tree, and to eat of its fruit in every season of our life and to live! By doing so, we will never again be the victim of sin, weaknesses and mistakes. Instead, we can stretch out our hands to the heart of God, where Mercy dwells, and bring forth a power from Him that far exceeds the weaknesses of humanity. This powerful help is as huge as the compassionate heart of the One who is in love with us.

I hear the heartbeat of the Father: "Mercy is yours!".

17 Therefore, if anyone [is] in Christ, [he is] a new creation; old things have passed away; behold, all things have become new.

18 Now all things [are] of God, who has reconciled us to Himself through Jesus Christ, and has given us the ministry of reconciliation,

19 that is, that God was in Christ reconciling the world to Himself, not imputing their trespasses to them, and has committed to us the word of reconciliation.

20 Now then, we are ambassadors for Christ, as though God were pleading through us: we implore [you] on Christ's behalf, be reconciled to God.

21 For He made Him who knew no sin [to be] sin for us, that we might become the righteousness of God in Him. [2 Corinthians 5:17-21]

About the Author

Rose Ramandi and her husband, Masoud, were both born and raised in Muslim families. Despite living accomplished lives filled with success and achievements attained through their mere human wisdom, desires and intellect, their lives felt confused. They were not seeing any meaning for life; they did not know their origin or the purpose of their creation.

In desperate need of finding the truth, they began reading the Bible and shortly thereafter encountered the truth that they were yearning for: "Jesus Christ". What they found in Him was marvellous. His Love was unconditional; His personality, wonderful; and the purpose of His coming, Glorious!

They whole-heartedly and joyfully bowed their knees to the One who filled their every void with Himself and kindled a passionate hunger to know Him intimately.

Masoud and Rose are passionate about revealing His mysteries and helping others know and see Him; not dimly, but rather, with certain clarity and brightness, beholding His Face as in a mirror and being transformed to the same image - the image of the Lord from Heaven.

For More Information:

www.PerfectedByBlood.com

contact@perfectedbyblood.com

Made in the USA
Columbia, SC
12 February 2020

87605239R00095